Jack C. Richards & Chuck Sandy

An upper-level multi-skills course

Passages

CAMBRIDGE
UNIVERSITY PRESS

Workbook 2

PUBLISHED BY THE PRESS SYNDICATE OF THE UNIVERSITY OF CAMBRIDGE
The Pitt Building, Trumpington Street, Cambridge, United Kingdom

CAMBRIDGE UNIVERSITY PRESS
The Edinburgh Building, Cambridge CB2 2RU, UK
40 West 20th Street, New York, NY 10011–4211, USA
10 Stamford Road, Oakleigh, Melbourne 3166, Australia
Ruiz de Alarcón 13, 28014 Madrid, Spain
Dock House, The Waterfront, Cape Town 8001, South Africa

http://www.cambridge.org

First published 2000
Third printing 2000

Printed in the United Kingdom at the University Press, Cambridge

Typeface Baskerville Book   *System* QuarkXPress®   [AH]

A catalog record for this book is available from the British Library

ISBN 0 521 56472 7 Student's Book 1
ISBN 0 521 56470 0 Workbook 1
ISBN 0 521 56468 9 Teacher's Manual 1
ISBN 0 521 56466 2 Class Audio Cassettes 1
ISBN 0 521 56464 6 Class Audio CDs 1
ISBN 0 521 56471 9 Student's Book 2
ISBN 0 521 56469 7 Workbook 2
ISBN 0 521 56467 0 Teacher's Manual 2
ISBN 0 521 56465 4 Class Audio Cassettes 2
ISBN 0 521 56463 8 Class Audio CDs 2

Book design, art direction, photo research, and layout services: Adventure House, NYC
Illustrators: Adventure House, Tom Barrett, Adam Hurwitz, Jonathan Keegan,
George Thompson, Bill Thomson, Daniel Vasconcellos

Contents

ILLUSTRATIONS

Tom Barrett   31, 41, 65
Adam Hurwitz   12, 32
Jonathan Keegan   20, 47, 58
George Thompson   8, 43, 53, 68
Bill Thomson   23, 50
Daniel Vasconcellos   10, 26, 35, 59

PHOTOGRAPHIC CREDITS

1 © M.K. Denny/PhotoEdit

6 © Deborah Feingold/Outline

7 (*left*) © Paul Barton/The Stock Market;
(*right*) © B. Seitz/Photo Researchers

8 © Jon Feingersh/The Stock Market

14 (*clockwise, from top right*) © Philip & Karen Smith/
Tony Stone Images; © Jose L. Palaez/The Stock Market;
© Robert Brenner/PhotoEdit; © Ariel Skelley/The Stock
Market; © Pete Saloutos/The Stock Market; © Gale
Zucker/Stock Boston

15 (*top*) © Bettman/Corbis;
(*bottom*) © Juergen Schwartz/Archive Photos

17 (*left to right*) © Alain Morvan/Liaison Agency; © AP/Wide
World Photos; © Liaison Agency; © AP/Wide World Photos

19 © FPG

22 © Archive Photos

27 (*top*) © Novastock/PhotoEdit;
(*bottom*) © Tony Freeman/PhotoEdit

38 © Image Bank

45 (*top to bottom*) © Paul Barton/The Stock Market; © Michael
Newman/PhotoEdit; © Jon Riley/Tony Stone Images

49 © Gail Mooney/Corbis

51 (*left*) © Lowell Georgia/Photo Researchers;
(*right*) © Gerard Champlong/Image Bank

56 © Jose Palaez/The Stock Market

61 © Wolfgang Kaehler/Corbis

62 © Alan R. Moller/Tony Stone Images

71 © Walter Hodges/Tony Stone Images

TEXT CREDITS

The authors and publishers are grateful for permission
to reprint the following items:

6 Interview with Dr. Joy Browne, author of *Dating for
Dummies*, February 13, 1998, on www.bn.com
Copyright © 1998 barnesandnoble.com
Reprinted by permission.

12 "Decoding Body Language" by John Mole, HYPERLINK
http://www.johnmole.com
Copyright © 1999. Reprinted by permission.

18 "Distinguished Service: Médecins Sans Frontières Receives
the Nobel Peace Prize" by Thomas Sancton, *Time*, October 25,
1999, vol. 154, no. 17. Copyright © 1999 Time Inc. New Media.

24 From the book titled *Dogwatching* by Desmond Morris,
Copyright © 1986 by Desmond Morris. Reprinted by permission
of Crown Publishers, a division of Random House, Inc.

30 "At Home, the TV Rules" by Steve Payne, *The Toronto Sun*,
November 25, 1999. Copyright © 1999 *The Toronto Sun*.
Reprinted with the permission of *The Toronto Sun*.

36 "Study Suggests Music May Someday Help Repair Brain" by
Robert Lee Hotz, *Los Angeles Times,* November 9, 1998, p. A1.
Copyright © 1998 *Los Angeles Times*.

42 "You; Getting Ready for Your 100th" by Don Oldenburg, *The
Washington Post*, August 10, 1999, p. CO4. Copyright © 1999
The Washington Post. Reprinted with permission.

48 "Behaviour Study on 'Shopaholics'" by Yvonne Martin, *The
Press*, August 2, 1999, p. 4. Copyright © 1999 The Christchurch
Press Company Limited, New Zealand. Reprinted by
permission.

54 "Fairy Tale Comes True" by Alexandar S. Dragicevic, *The
Toronto Star*, July 12, 1998. Copyright © 1998 Associated
Press.

60 "Dialects" by Margelit Fox, *New York Times Magazine*,
September 12, 1999. Copyright © 1999 The New York Times
Company.

66 "The Soybean" by Peter Warshall and Imhoff Dan, Whole
Earth, summer 1999. Copyright © 1999 Whole Earth.

72 "New Variations on Recruitment Prescreening" by Mary
Helen Yarborough, *HR Focus*, October 1, 1994, pp. 1 (3), vol.
71. Copyright © 1994 American Management Association.

Every effort has been made to trace the owners of the copyright
material in this book. We would be grateful to hear from
anyone who recognizes his or her copyright material and who
is unacknowledged. We will be pleased to make the necessary
corrections in future editions of the book.

Lesson A

The best of friends

1

grammar

Read this paragraph from a composition about friendship. Find the phrasal verbs, and write them in the correct column in the chart.

> Pablo was a friend to many people, but he and I got along especially well. If I had a problem, I knew that I could always go to him to talk it over. Just talking to him would cheer me up. Once he helped me get over my disappointment when I didn't make the football team. Another time, he stuck up for a friend who was falsely accused of cheating on an exam. I sometimes wondered how he put up with me because sometimes I wasn't so nice to other people. But Pablo would never let a friend down. After high school, we both moved away to go to college, but we have stayed in touch.

Separable	Inseparable	Intransitive
		got along

2

grammar

Complete these dialogs. Use the correct form of the phrasal verbs in the box.

get along	make up	put up with	run into	stand by	talk over

1. A: I'm surprised that Tom didn't support what you said in the meeting. I thought he agreed with you.

   B: He does agree with me, but he was afraid of what the boss would say. I can't believe he didn't _____*stand by*_____ me!

2. A: I see that Judy's late again. She's going to lose her job if she's not careful.

   B: You two are friends. Maybe you should _____ it _____ with her.

3. A: What do you think of Amelia?

   B: I _____ with her very well. Maybe we should ask her to go to the movies with us sometime.

4. A: Sam isn't serious about anything. How do you _____ him?

   B: Well, he's my friend. He's done a lot of nice things for me.

5. A: Have you seen Cynthia Clark lately?

   B: As a matter of fact, I _____ her when I was downtown today.

6. A: Is it true that you and Roger got into a big argument?

   B: Yes, but he called to apologize, and we _____ .

1

3

grammar

Rewrite each sentence using one of the phrasal verbs in the box.

get along	let down	put up with	stick up for
get over	make up	run into	talk over

1. Suzanne unexpectedly met an old high school friend on the subway this morning.
   Suzanne ran into an old high school friend on the subway this morning.

2. It took me a few days to overcome my anger.

3. Marcia and Alice are roommates, but they don't like each other.

4. Karl finds it difficult to tolerate my smoking when we're together.

5. A good friend will support you when you've been falsely accused.

6. Can we discuss a problem that I have at work?

7. Mark and Ying had a big fight about politics, but they soon became friends again.

8. Linda disappointed Tom when she didn't meet him at the airport as she had promised.

4

grammar

Complete these sentences to make them true for you.

1. Nothing cheers me up as much as

2. I get along best with people who

3. When someone lets me down, I

4. I will stick up for friends when

5. My friends have to put up with me when

6. When I drift apart from a friend, I

writing

A Read the thesis statements. Then find the three best paragraph topics in the box to support each one. Write the topics below the thesis statements.

Thesis statements

1. Developing a friendship requires attention and work.

   Be a person that your friend can trust.

   _____

   _____

2. People living in big cities often have trouble making friends, but there are ways to solve this problem.

   _____

   _____

   _____

3. Maintaining a friendship over distance is difficult, but it can be done.

   _____

   _____

   _____

Paragraph topics

✔ Be a person that your friend can trust.
✔ Join clubs and other organizations that relate to your special interests or hobbies.
✔ Know when to give advice and when to keep silent.
✔ Use the telephone or send messages by E-mail.
✔ Sign up for a class, such as painting or cooking.
✔ Participate in community service activities, such as working with the elderly.
✔ Pay attention to what your friend thinks and feels.
✔ Get together and travel whenever possible.
✔ Use the mail: write letters, send birthday and holiday cards, send inexpensive presents.

B Write one additional paragraph topic for each thesis statement.

1. _____

2. _____

3. _____

C Choose one of the thesis statements above, and write a composition.
Use the three paragraph topics that best support your thesis.

Lesson B *More than a friend*

1

grammar

Read these personal ads. Underline the verb + gerund constructions, and circle the verb + infinitive constructions.

My name is Naomi. I'm 25, and I'm a lawyer. I like to go out with people who enjoy playing sports and who intend to be successful in life. Write to me if you want to be taken seriously! Box WA-1468.

Hello! I'm a

I've just moved here, and I'm looking for some new friends. I love spending quiet evenings at home cooking, listening to music, and talking. I certainly don't mind going out, either, especially to movies. I'm a great cook – if you want to be treated to a great meal, let me hear from you. Write to Ryan. Box TW-4361.

Box TR-2309.
I'm Alex, and I'm seeking someone who really prefers living in the city. I love having a good time – dinner, dancing, and maybe a nightclub act. And . . . I like to stay out until the sun comes up! Box TR-2310.

2

grammar

Complete these questions using the gerund or infinitive form of the verbs. Note that some of the constructions use the passive voice. Then answer the questions.

1. Do you hope _____*to get*_____ (get) married within the next five years?

   _____

2. Would you refuse _____ (date) someone five years older or five years younger than you?

   _____

3. Would you consider _____ (go) out with someone from a different culture?

   _____

4. Do you enjoy _____ (take) to expensive places?

   _____

5. Would you prefer _____ (invite) to a basketball game or to a movie?

   _____

6. On a date, do you mind _____ (take) public transportation?

   _____

7. On a first date, do you expect _____ (learn) a lot about the other person?

   _____

8. Would you ask _____ (take) home if you weren't having a good time?

   _____

3

grammar

Read this E-mail message from a close friend you are planning to visit. Then write a response that is true for you using some of the verbs in the box.

| avoid | enjoy | hate | like | love | plan | prefer |

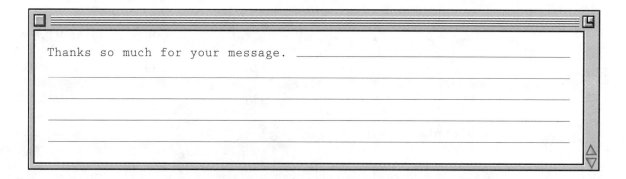

I can't wait to see you this Saturday! I've been thinking about what we can do that night. First, maybe you'd like to go for a walk along the river. Then we could have dinner at my favorite French restaurant. It's formal - we'd have to dress up. There's also a great Vietnamese restaurant in the same area that is more informal. After dinner, we could go to a dance club, or maybe a quieter jazz club. Do you have any other ideas? This city is small, but there's a lot of variety. Let me know what you'd like to do, and I'll try to find it.

Thanks so much for your message. _____

_____

_____

_____

_____

4

vocabulary

Apply the words in the box to each situation.

| disastrous | embarrassing | hilarious | intriguing | tense |

1. _____tense_____ Anne and Roger had tickets for the theater. When they got to their seats, another couple was sitting in them and refused to move.

2. _____ Sue received a dozen red roses yesterday. The card read, "From your admirer." She seems to know who sent the roses, but her friends don't.

3. _____ Pedro and Karen went on a picnic last weekend. They had a flat tire on the way to the park. When they got there, it was raining. Then Karen got stung by a bee. They had an awful time.

4. _____ Ko asked Teresa to go to a soccer game with him. It was their first date. When they got to the stadium, he discovered that he'd left the tickets at home.

5. _____ When Tony got back from France, he told everyone about the misunderstandings that arose when he tried to speak French. Everyone laughed until they cried.

reading

A Write your own short answers to these questions. Then read this excerpt of an interview with the psychotherapist Joy Browne, an author and TV/radio personality.

1. Is it a good idea to date people you meet over the Internet? _____

2. How do you get someone to notice you? _____

3. What's the best way to meet people? _____

4. Is "love at first sight" possible? _____

5. Should a woman always turn down the first invitation for a date? _____

Question: What do you think of dating over the Internet?

Dr. Joy Browne: I generally don't advocate dating people you've met on-line. There's too much fantasy involved and not enough reality. Meeting someone on-line is OK for a bit of spice or fantasy, but to love someone you have to actually know them, not the fantasy of who you'd like them to be.

Question: I was wondering, what is the easiest way to let someone know you exist?

Dr. Joy Browne: Make eye contact, smile, flirt – unless it's at work, and then I would suggest you wait until one of you leaves the company, since work is about competence, and dating is about fun. Try being friendly and charming rather than overly flirtatious. I'll bet they do know you exist.

Question: I'm 29 and having a hard time meeting someone my age. Any advice?

Dr. Joy Browne: Try meeting people in ordinary places like church or grocery stores or my favorite, volunteer activities. Maybe you're asking too many questions too soon. Women trust you and may unload on you. Try lightening up a bit on dates and doing fun, casual stuff, and see if that works better for you.

Question: What do you think of "love at first sight"?

Dr. Joy Browne: I think love at first sight is chemistry with potential. Far be it from me to bad-mouth, either, but it's not love. You can't love someone you can't trust, and you don't know someone until you've had enough time to learn to trust them. It's fun and exciting, but it's chemistry. It takes at least a couple of months to really know someone enough to know it's love. But enjoy the chemistry, just don't bank on it.

Question: Is it proper for a woman to turn down the first invitation for a date?

Dr. Joy Browne: If you don't want to go out, sure. When in doubt, give somebody the benefit of that doubt. But if you're playing games or playing hard to get, it's a lousy idea to start off on a dishonest foot. A rejection doesn't feel very good to either sex. If you want to go, go. If not, politely decline – but no games, please.

B Read these answers to the questions in the interview. Check agree (**A**) if the answer matches Dr. Browne's opinion and disagree (**D**) if it doesn't.

	A	D
1. You shouldn't get too involved with people you meet on the Internet.	☐	☐
2. To get someone to notice you, you should do things like sending flowers.	☐	☐
3. The best way to meet people is through everyday, casual activities.	☐	☐
4. "Love at first sight" is fun and exciting, but it's not true love.	☐	☐
5. You should always turn someone down who asks you out for the first time.	☐	☐

Lesson A   *The way we dress*

vocabulary

Match the words with their definitions. Then complete the sentences.

casual — traditional
conservative — careless; not neat
chic — comfortable and informal
sloppy — highly individual; odd
eccentric — in keeping with the latest trends of fashion

1. At a picnic, I'd wear _____*casual*_____ clothes.

2. If I were going dancing at the fanciest club in town, I'd wear something _____ .

3. I'd wear a _____ suit to a job interview at a bank.

4. If I were going to a costume party, I'd get something _____ .

5. When I'm alone at home, I can wear _____ clothes if I want.

grammar

Match the sentences to tell the story of Mimi, a fashion designer in Tokyo.

1. When I was a small child, I enjoyed __*i*__

2. As I got a little older, I wanted ___

3. When I was a teenager, my parents permitted ___

4. My mother recognized my interest in clothing, and she encouraged ___

5. By the time I graduated from high school, I knew that I would try ___

6. My teachers recommended ___

7. I thought that the high cost of the school would prevent ___

8. Fortunately, I got a scholarship that allowed ___

9. Now, five years after graduating, I'm a fashion designer. I love ___

a. designing beautiful clothes for the best shops in Japan!

b. going to a fashion school in New York City.

c. me from going there.

d. me to buy what I wanted.

e. me to learn more about it.

f. me to study there for four years.

g. to make my own choices.

h. to work in the fashion industry.

i. wearing what other people bought for me.

3

grammar

Read what Kevin said to some co-workers about clothes and fashion. Use the gerund or the infinitive form of the verbs in parentheses.

If you ask me, I think people are just trying ___*to impress*___ (impress) other people when they wear expensive clothes. It's a waste of money. You can manage ___*to look*___ (look) neat and well-dressed much less expensively if you avoid ___*buying*___ (buy) clothing from the big designers. There are too many serious problems in the world. I would discourage people from ___*spending*___ (spend) money on luxuries like fancy clothes and encourage them ___*to donate*___ (donate) more of their money to charities!

4

grammar

What kind of dress code should there be at your school? Use the verbs in the box to write sentences that express your opinion.

| advise | allow | avoid | discourage | permit | tell | want |

1. _I think schools should advise sts to wear uniform._
2. _Schools should discourage sts. to wear casual expensive clothes_
3. _____
4. _____
5. _____
6. _____
7. _____

writing

A Underline the thesis statements in these introductory paragraphs. Then complete the paragraphs that follow with examples supporting each thesis statement.

> Getting dressed up can be a lot of fun if you have the right attitude. Many people despise dressing up and can't wait to get back into their jeans and sweatshirts, but I love putting on my best clothes. I plan what I am going to wear very carefully.
>
> I like to dress nicely for many different types of occasions. For example, . . .
>
> _____
> _____
> _____
>
> There are many advantages to dressing nicely. For example, . . .
>
> _____
> _____
> _____

> Teenagers spend a significant portion of their income on the "right clothes." For many, following the newest trends in an effort to fit in can become an obsession. I feel that young people need to reject pressure to dress stylishly.
>
> Keeping up with the latest fashions is an expensive pursuit. For example, . . .
>
> _____
> _____
> _____
>
> Television and fashion magazines do not set a good example. They . . .
>
> _____
> _____
> _____

B Choose one of these topics to write about. Write a thesis statement that expresses your own point of view.

1. There _____ many advantages to dressing casually at work. (are/aren't)

2. Teenagers _____ be required to wear school uniforms. (should/shouldn't)

3. Employees _____ be judged by what they wear. (should/shouldn't)

_____
_____

C Make a list of examples that support your thesis statement.

_____
_____
_____
_____

D Use your thesis statement and examples to develop a composition containing an introductory paragraph and at least two supporting paragraphs.

grammar

Read the diary entry, and underline the cleft sentences.

December 9

Dear Diary,

Today at the gym, I met this great person. She was using the stair machine next to mine. What I noticed first was the look of determination on her face. She was really working hard! As she was finishing up, I started chatting with her and asked what her name was. It was Susie. We talked some more, and what I really liked was her sense of humor. Then she asked me what exercise I was going to do next.

I told her I was finished. She said she was also finished, and she asked me to have something to drink with her at the juice bar. So, we had a great time for about an hour. What struck me most about her was her assertiveness. I think she's a very strong person — emotionally — and I like that. But I made a big mistake. I forgot to ask for her phone number! What am I going to do? I guess I'll have to go back to the gym every day until I see her again. What I can't believe is how stupid I was!

grammar

Read what each person thinks about the world-famous fashion model Gina Riccardi, who had an appointment at an advertising agency today. Then complete the dialog using cleft sentences with *noticed*, *liked*, *admired*, or *struck me*.

Jin: She's as beautiful in person as she is in her ads.

Dolores: She is beautiful, but _what I noticed first was that beautiful dress!_
　　　　　　　　　　　　　　　　　　　　　　　　　　　　　　　1

Brian: Not me. _____ How about you, Jin?
　　　　　　　　　　　　　2

Jin: Yes, her eyes are stunning, but _____
　　　　　　　　　　　　　　　　　　　　　　　　3

Ted: As for me, _____
　　　　　　　　　　　　　　　4

Brian: Her voice? Come on, Ted. She's a fashion model, not a singer!

3

grammar

Imagine you are hiring a new employee. What personal characteristics do you look for? Use your own ideas to complete these sentences.

1. What I look for in an employee is _____

   _____

2. What I think is most important is _____

   _____

3. What I probably notice first is _____

   _____

4. What I pay attention to is _____

   _____

5. What I ask about first is _____

   _____

6. What I think is least important is _____

   _____

4

vocabulary

Choose the correct word to complete these sentences.

1. An older woman, dressed in black, came into our meeting and sat down. She took notes for about five minutes and, without saying a word, left the room. None of us had ever seen her before. She was very _____ . (kind/mysterious/dignified)

2. When I went into the ambassador's office, he rose from his desk. He was about 60, and he wore a classic suit that was obviously very expensive. He had a calm, serious manner, and when he spoke, his voice was firm but not unkind. Everything in his manner made me treat him with the greatest respect. In short, he was the most _____ man I had ever met. (sinister/trustworthy/dignified)

3. As the girl played a computer game, she sat forward in her chair. Her eyes were glued to the screen. Her hands gripped the game controls tightly as she directed the action on-screen. Later, her mother told me that she is equally _____ in everything that she does.   (intense/striking/severe)

4. Feeling very nervous, I entered my boss's office and sat down across from him. I explained that the project that I had been working on was going to be late because of some errors that I'd made. His reaction surprised me. Rather than getting angry, he just asked me how I was going to correct the situation and prevent it from happening again. Then he said that it wasn't all my fault. I can't believe he was so _____ .   (self-satisfied/intelligent/sympathetic)

5. On the train the other day, a woman was telling someone about her family. She said that her husband had the most important job in his company and that her children went to the most prestigious schools. She also claimed to live in the best neighborhood in the city. How could someone be so _____ ? (severe/forbidding/arrogant)

A Read this article on body language. Do any of the behaviors discussed apply to your culture?

UNDERSTANDING BODY LANGUAGE

In European and North American cultures, body language behaviors can be divided into two groups: open/closed and forward/back.

Open/closed postures are the easiest to recognize. People are open to messages when they show open hands, face you fully, and have both feet on the ground. This indicates that they are willing to listen to what you have to say, even if they are disagreeing with you. When people are closed to messages, they have their arms folded or their legs crossed, and they may turn their bodies away. This body language usually means that people are rejecting your message.

Forward/back behavior reveals an active or a passive reaction to what is being said. If people lean forward with their bodies toward you, they are actively engaged in your message. They may be accepting or rejecting it, but their minds are on what you are saying. On the other hand, if people lean back in their chairs or look away from you, or perform activities such as drawing or cleaning their eyeglasses, you know that they are either passively taking in your message or that they are ignoring it. In either case, they are not very much engaged in the conversation.

The chart below shows how these types of body language can suggest the general mental state of the listener.

Open

Responsive: The person is willing to listen to you (open) and wants to participate in the conversation (forward).

Reflective: The person is willing to listen (open) but not to share his or her opinion (back). He or she wants more time to think.

Forward ——————————————— **Back**

Combative: There is risk of an argument. The person is engaged in the conversation (forward) but rejects your message (closed).

Fugitive: The person is trying to avoid the conversation. He or she does not want to be a part of the conversation (back) and is rejecting your message (closed).

Closed

B Check the qualities that apply to each body language type.

	willing to listen	not willing to listen	engaged in conversation	not engaged in conversation
1. responsive	☐	☐	☐	☐
2. reflective	☐	☐	☐	☐
3. combative	☐	☐	☐	☐
4. fugitive	☐	☐	☐	☐

C Write the body language type under each picture.

responsive
reflective
combative
fugitive

fugitive

reflective

responsive

combative

High achievers

1

grammar

Rewrite these sentences using compound adjectives. More than one answer is possible.

1. Marta is a model with curly hair and brown eyes.

   Marta is a curly-haired, brown-eyed model.

2. In my opinion, diplomats must be open to other people's ideas.

   In my opinion, diplomats must be opened minded

3. I was confused by the salesman, who was talking too fast.

   I was confused by the saterman who was a fast-talking

4. Maxwell's is a restaurant not many people know about.

   Maxwell's is a little-known restaurant

5. The famous conductor is recognized by many people.

   The famous Conductor is wildly-recognized

6. Dr. Kendall is a teacher who looks very intelligent.

   Dr. Kendall is a forward-looking

7. Sonya made a good first impression at the interview because she was dressed so well.

   Sonya made a good first impression at the interview because she was well-dressed.

2

grammar

Make compound adjectives to fit the descriptions. Then write the adjectives in the blanks.

closed	educated
easy	fashioned
good	going
high	looking
old	minded
poorly	read
strong	spirited
well	willed

This is a word used to describe a person . . .

1. who has had a lot of exposure to important literature. _____*well-read*_____

2. who is considered attractive. *good-looking*

3. who did not receive much schooling. *poorly-educated*

4. who is relaxed and casual. *easy-going*

5. who is not considered modern. *old-fashioned*

6. who is determined to do something in his or her own way. *strong-willed*

7. who does not want to consider the ideas of other people. *close-minded*

8. who has a lively and energetic character. *high-spirited*

3 What qualities should these people have? Write a sentence using two compound adjectives.

social worker

mountain climber

1. *A social worker should be* high-spirited *and thought-provoking person.*

2. _____

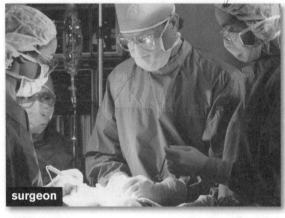

surgeon

judge

3. _____

4. _____

car salesman

clown

5. _____

6. _____

A Read this biography of composer and conductor Leonard Bernstein. Then answer the questions below.

♪♪♪♪ *Leonard Bernstein* ♪♪♪

Leonard Bernstein was perhaps the single greatest figure in American classical music in the twentieth century. Born in 1918 in Lawrence, Massachusetts, he studied piano as a child in Boston. 1 Upon his graduation from Harvard in 1939, he went to Philadelphia to study at the Curtis Institute. 2 By the time Bernstein finished his training, he was widely respected as a major talent in the music world. 3

In 1943, Bernstein became the assistant conductor of the New York Philharmonic. One night, he was asked to substitute for a conductor who was sick. This was a particularly difficult concert, but Bernstein performed brilliantly and was a great success. 4 Over the next 15 years, he held conducting positions in several of the great orchestras of the world, and he performed as a guest conductor with many others. His work included both live concerts and recordings. 5

In 1958, Bernstein became the music director of the New York Philharmonic. That same year, he started a series of televised programs called *Young People's Concerts*, designed to teach children an appreciation for great music. At the Philharmonic, Bernstein was a very popular conductor. He brought new music to the orchestra, and he revitalized older music that hadn't been played for some time. 6

Bernstein died in New York City in 1990. He was conducting and composing music up until the time of his death. Through his lifetime of conducting, composing, teaching, and helping people understand music, he left a great gift to the world.

1. In what year did Leonard Bernstein leave Harvard University? _1939_

2. How long did Bernstein conduct orchestras all over the world before he became the music director of the New York Philharmonic? _15 years_

3. In what year did Bernstein start *Young People's Concerts*? _1958_

B There are six boxes in the biography. Find where each of the following sentences should go, and write the number of the box beside the sentence.

a. _6_ In 1969, Bernstein left the New York Philharmonic and spent the remaining years of his life composing a wide variety of music, conducting all over the world, and teaching young musicians.

b. _1_ At the age of 17, he entered Harvard University, where he studied composition.

c. _____ During his years there, he spent his summers at the Boston Symphony Orchestra's summer institute at Tanglewood, in Massachusetts, where he studied with the conductor Serge Koussevitzky.

C Choose someone you admire who has made a difference in people's lives. Research the key facts of the person's life, and write a three-paragraph biography.

Lesson B *Personal heroes*

1

grammar

Read the journal entry, and underline the superlative adjectives.

> Without a doubt, my most memorable teacher was Mr. Hill, my college French professor. He was a gentle man and showed concern for his students, so he was the teacher who made us feel the most comfortable in class. He always came to class with lessons that made me want to learn, so he was also the most motivating teacher I've ever had. When he taught us to speak, he was very good. He truly loved French culture, so for me, the cultural lessons were the most inspiring. He made me feel that I was looking through a window into another world, and he made me want to be a part of that world. I guess I never learned much French — it's not the easiest language — but I did learn how good a teacher can be and how rewarding it can be to learn about another culture.

2

grammar

Read these dialogs and fill in the first blank with the superlative form of the adjectives in parentheses. Fill in the second blank with a relative clause to add more information.

1. Pete: What did you think of the boss's speech?

   Mindy: I thought it was _the most thought-provoking_ speech _I'd ever heard_ . (thought-provoking)

2. Sung-Ho: Don't you think Tom is funny?

   Danny: Yes. Of all my friends, I think he's _the wittiest_ person _I've ever seen_ . (witty)

3. Bruce: What do you think is _the bravest_ thing _you've ever seen_ ? (brave)

   Valerie: I once saw a lifeguard save a surfer. The waves were enormous!

4. Rick: I really like your aunt Carmen.

   Linda: I'm glad you do. She is _the most inspiring_ relative _I've ever had_ . (inspiring)

5. Paul: I heard that Bob has volunteered to help out disadvantaged kids in the city.

   Sarah: That doesn't surprise me. Bob is one of _the most kindhearted_ people _I've ever seen_ . (kindhearted)

6. Mick: Do you think Joseph is telling the truth?

   Yuri: Of course he is. He's _the most honest_ person _I've ever seen_ . (honest)

3

grammar

What people do you most admire? Write sentences about some of these public figures or people of your own choosing. Use superlative adjectives in your sentences.

Kofi Annan, Secretary-General of the United Nations **Isabel Allende, best-selling author** **Lu Chen, Olympic figure skater** **Tiger Woods, champion golfer**

1. *I admire Kofi Annan because he is one of the most fair-minded world leaders I have ever seen.*

2. *I admire Isabel Allende she's one of the most thought-provoking person I've ever seen.*

3. *I admire Lu Chen she is the most talented skater I've ever seen.*

4. *I admire tiger woods he's one of the most accurate golf players in the world.*

4

vocabulary

Write a response to each question. Use the phrasal verbs in the box.

calm (someone) down	follow through on (something)	pick (something) up
check on (someone/something)	give (something) away	

1. You are helping a friend set up his computer, and you realize you are missing your favorite television program. What should you do?
   I should follow through on it

2. An elderly person in the supermarket has dropped a heavy box on the floor and wants to put it into his or her shopping cart. What should you do?
   I should pick it up and put it into her shopping

3. You see that someone is very upset. What should you do?
   I should calm him down

4. A friend has the flu and lives alone. What should you do?
   I should check on him

5. You have a lot of clothes that you don't wear anymore. What should you do with them?
   I should give them away

A Read this article about Médecins Sans Frontières (MSF), or Doctors Without Borders. Then check the adjectives that describe the organization.

- ☑ Oslo-based
- ☐ overly bureaucratic
- ☑ award-winning
- ☐ narrow-minded
- ☑ internationally minded

Distinguished Service

Shortly before the winner of the 1999 Nobel Peace Prize was announced, staffers at the Paris headquarters of Médecins Sans Frontières – Doctors Without Borders – played down their chances. "We've been nominated so many times already," said one, "but we're always passed over." Not this time. The Oslo-based Nobel committee named the crusading medical and humanitarian organization as its newest peace laureate.

The committee's statement praised the 28-year-old group for its "pioneering humanitarian work on several continents" and for championing "the fundamental principle that all disaster victims, whether the disaster is natural or human in origin, have a right to professional assistance given as quickly and as efficiently as possible." The prestigious $975,000 award was quite a recompense for what started as a ragtag band of antiestablishment French doctors. It has since grown into an international network with 23 offices, fielding 2,000 medical volunteers in 80 countries and commanding an annual budget of $167 million – nearly 80% of which comes from private donations.

MSF has always asserted its independence from governments or large bureaucratic organizations like the International Red Cross. In fact, it was created largely as a reaction to the Red Cross approach of strict neutrality and respect for diplomatic niceties. "International relief agencies were too respectful of notions of noninterference and sovereignty," recalls MSF cofounder Rony Brauman. "When we saw people dying on the other side of the frontiers, we asked ourselves, 'What is this border? It doesn't mean anything to us.'"

While the Red Cross would only enter a crisis zone with local government permission and forbade its volunteers and staffers to take political stands, the founders of MSF were activists who insisted on a "duty to interfere" in troubled areas and to speak out about what they saw. "The movement was political from the start," explained cofounder Bernard Kouchner. "The tradition was medical, the action was medical, but we had to convince people that borders should not protect disgraceful conduct and suffering."

B Check whether each statement applies to MSF or to the Red Cross.

	MSF	Red Cross
1. It started as a small, informal group of doctors.	☑	☐
2. It received the Nobel Prize in 1999.	☑	☐
3. It pays attention to diplomatic concerns.	☐	☑
4. It waits for local governments' permission before entering crisis zones.	☐	☑
5. It tries to make political points.	☑	☐

Lesson A   *Superstitions*

1

Choose the correct words to complete these sentences.

vocabulary

1. People who avoid black cats do so because they _____*claim*_____ that these animals bring bad luck.   (claim/explain)

2. Folklorists _____*explain*_____ that people used to believe that evil spirits entered the body when we yawned. That's why we still cover our mouths when we yawn – to keep the evil spirits out.   (doubt/explain)

3. Some people _____*doubt*_____ that superstitions are true, but they continue to believe in them anyway.   (doubt/assume)

4. Some older people in the United States continue to _____*admit*_____ that a cat can take the breath away from a baby, even though there is no evidence that this is true.   (admit/assert)

5. People who believe in many superstitions may _____*feel*_____ that they have no control over their lives.   (feel/doubt)

6. Superstitions usually have deep roots in a particular culture. It is a mistake to _____*admit*_____ that they don't mean anything.   (admit/assume)

7. Researchers into superstitions might _____*report.*_____ that more people are superstitious than we think.   (believe/report)

2

Underline the reporting clauses in this paragraph.

grammar

The care of babies is the subject of many superstitions in the United States. For example, <u>some parents say</u> that something is wrong if their baby gets his or her teeth late. But <u>scientists assert</u> that late teething is irrelevant to physical or mental growth. <u>Some people believe</u> that babies who are frightened by strangers will be insecure. This is simply untrue, according to child psychologists. <u>Some parents believe</u> that their babies will walk faster if they wear shoes. <u>The experts say</u> that this, too, is a myth – babies who go barefoot develop their muscles more rapidly. What about fat babies? Traditionally, <u>people have assumed</u> that fat babies are healthy, but <u>today's research reports</u> that they tend to become overweight adults. Parents who want the best for their children should pay attention to the facts rather than blindly following superstitions.

grammar

Combine each pair of sentences using the words in parentheses.

1. As a child, I believed some strange things. A monster was living under my bed.   (believe)

   As I child, I _____ *believed* _____ a monster *was living under my bed.*

2. To keep it away, I had to do certain things. I had to adjust the covers over me.   (feel)

   To keep it away, I _____ *felt* _____ I *had to do certain things to adjust the covers over me*

3. I needed extra help. My stuffed bear would protect me.   (assume)

   I _____ *assumed* _____ my stuffed bear *would protect me*

4. I was sure of one thing. My parents wouldn't understand about the monster.   (doubt)

   I _____ *doubted* _____ my parents *would understand about the monster.*

grammar

Use the verbs in parentheses to explain what you would do in these situations.

1. Your friend won't travel on Friday the thirteenth because he considers it to be an unlucky day. How would you reassure him?   (explain)

   I would explain that Friday the thirteenth is just like any other day.

2. Your boss saw you rubbing a rabbit's foot for good luck. How would you explain this?   (admit)

   _____

3. You aren't superstitious, but your friend claims that observing some superstitions brings good luck. How would you respond?   (argue)

   I would argue that superstitions don't bring luck.

4. Your friend always carries good luck charms with her. How would you explain this?   (assume)

   _____

5. You read an article about how the names given to Chinese babies are carefully chosen to be lucky. How would you tell someone about this article?   (report)

   _____

5

writing

A Read the composition and answer the questions by filling in each blank with the letter of the appropriate sentence.

1. Which sentence is the thesis statement? _a_

2. Which sentence gives general examples? _b_

3. Which sentence reflects the author's personal belief about old wives' tales? _e_

4. Which sentence restates the thesis statement? _d_

[a] *Beliefs called "old wives' tales" are not the same as superstitions. They differ in that they supposedly transmit useful information from one generation to another.* [b] *For example, I'm sure most of us can remember our parents' telling us to eat certain foods or to avoid specific behaviors. Is there wisdom in these teachings, or are they without value?* [c] *Some of the old wives' tales passed down over the generations reflect current medical thinking, whereas others have not passed the test of time.*

Did your mother ever tell you to eat your carrots because they are good for your eyes? Scientists now report that eating carrots can help prevent a severe eye disease called macular degeneration. Because carrots are rich in a substance called beta carotene, eating just one carrot a day can reduce the likelihood of contracting this disease by 40%. Is garlic really good for you? It turns out that it is. It can kill the type of virus that causes colds. How about chicken soup? We now understand that chicken contains an amino acid that is similar to a drug often prescribed for people with respiratory infections.

Unfortunately, not all of Mom's advice has __withstood__ medical inquiry. For example, generations of children have been told not to go swimming for an hour after eating. But research suggests that there is no danger in having lunch and then diving back into the ocean. Is chocolate really so bad for the complexions of teenagers? Doctors now believe that there is little connection between diet and an outbreak of acne. Does candy cause tooth decay? Well, yes and no. Sticky candy or other sweets made with grains tend to cause more __decay__ than sweets made with simple sugars, which dissolve quickly in the mouth.

[d] *Even though science can persuade us that some of our traditional beliefs don't hold water, there is still a lot of wisdom in the old wives' tales that have been handed down from generation to generation.* [e] *After all, much of this lore has been accumulated from thousands of years of __trial-and-error__ experience in family health care.* [f] *We should respect this informal body of knowledge even as we search for clear scientific evidence to prove it true or false.*

B Write a composition about old wives' tales in your own culture. Tell about some you think are true, and some you think are not.

Lesson B *Believe it or not*

1

Underline the reporting verbs that are in the passive voice.

The War of the Worlds

On October 30, 1938, perhaps the most famous broadcast in the entire history of radio took place. Heard all over the United States, the broadcast reported that a spacecraft from Mars had landed in a small town in New Jersey. It was said that the Martians were attacking the surrounding area with a "death ray." Radio reporters also claimed that three huge war machines had emerged from the spacecraft. After much destruction, it was reported that the Martians were dying. Specialists suggested that the Martians had no resistance to Earth's infectious diseases.

Of course, this story was just a radio play, written and produced by a famous actor, Orson Welles, but many people believed it. It was reported that there was widespread panic throughout the country, especially in New Jersey. It has been suggested that Welles's broadcast offers many lessons about how the mass media can affect people.

2

Change the reporting verb in each sentence into the passive voice. Then write an additional sentence that expresses your opinion.

1. Many scientists argue that there is probably life on other planets.

   It is argued that there is probably life on other planets.

   _____

2. Astronomers believe that the universe began with a huge explosion.

   It's believed that the universe began with a huge explosion

3. Some people have claimed that John F. Kennedy's death was the result of a criminal conspiracy.

   It has been claimed that John F. Kennedy's death was the result of a criminal conspiracy.

4. Medical research suggests that traditional treatments such as acupuncture are very effective.

   It's suggested that traditional treatments such as acupuncture

5. Geologists have reported that animals can predict earthquakes.

   IT has been reported that animals can predict earthquakes. -

6. A recent study has shown that more than 60% of Americans believe that UFOs probably exist.

   It has been shown that more than 60% of americans believe that UFOs probably exist

3

grammar

Read the information about each person. Write a passive sentence using a reporting word from the box. Then answer the questions.

argue	claim	estimate	report	suggest

1. Ko has been a high-school teacher for three years. He has a college degree.

   In a faculty meeting yesterday, it was _argued that_ _studying English should be optional._ .

   Would you trust this opinion? ☐ Yes ☑ No ☐ Maybe

   Studying English should be optional.

2. Dr. Ortega is a biologist at a famous university. She is in charge of a large, government-funded research project.

   In a news release yesterday, it was _reported that there may be simple plant life on Venus._

   Would you trust this opinion? ☐ Yes ☐ No ☑ Maybe

   There may be simple plant life on Venus.

   $E = mc^2$

3. Madame Mona is an astrologist and a fortune-teller. She learned her skills from her famous grandmother.

   In a New Year's interview with Madame Mona, it was _claimed that all nations will be at peace._

   Would you trust this opinion? ☐ Yes ☑ No ☐ Maybe

   All nations will be at peace.

4. Fred grows plants in a greenhouse. He has been doing this for 35 years.

   In an agricultural journal last month, it was _suggested that plants grow better if classical music is played._

   Would you trust this opinion? ☑ Yes ☐ No ☐ Maybe

   Plants grow better if classical music is played.

4

vocabulary

Complete these sentences with words from the box.

astrology	ESP	ghost	psychic	telepathy

1. I don't believe in _astrology_ . Stars and planets surely can't influence us.

2. If you hear a strange noise at night, don't assume it's a _ghost_ .

3. Ken claims to gather information not from his five senses, but from _ESP_ .

4. The magician said he could read my mind using _telepathy_ .

5. I went to a _psychic_ once. Nothing she predicted came true.

A Read the article about the possible extrasensory perception of dogs. Match the ability with the explanation.

1. finding its way home _b_
2. predicting thunderstorms _a_
3. knowing if a buried person is alive or not _c_

a. changes in barometric pressure
b. changes in the earth's magnetic field
c. infrared heat sensors on the dog's snout

THE AMAZING ABILITIES OF DOGS

Do dogs have a sixth sense? Yes, but perhaps not in the way that is generally assumed. There is nothing supernatural about canine sensitivities. They can all be explained by biological mechanisms, although it is true that we are only beginning to understand some of them.

For instance, dogs can find their way home from long distances. This ability seems to be based on the detection of subtle differences and changes in the earth's magnetic field. We are still learning how dogs achieve such remarkable navigational feats as have been objectively recorded time and again.

Dogs are also capable of predicting thunderstorms. When a storm is imminent, they may become intensely alarmed and begin whimpering and trembling as if in pain. Their distress increases when the thunder starts to boom, but it can be observed for some time before the storm actually breaks overhead. This sensitivity is a response to changes in barometric pressure. It may seem to be meaningless behavior today, but in the dog's wild ancestry it made good sense to become worried by these climactic signals. For example, wolves go to a great deal of trouble to build their dens on slopes, perhaps to protect tiny pups from floods. It is possible that domestic dogs are acting out the behavior of their ancestors' response to the danger of flooding.

One of the most amazing claims for the dog's sixth sense was made recently by researchers who reported that they had discovered infrared detectors in the dog's nose. This could explain certain abilities previously thought to be supernatural. St. Bernard dogs, for example, are said to be able to tell whether a climber buried in an avalanche is still alive, simply by sniffing the snow. If there are sensitive heat detectors in the noses of animals, this theory is not so far-fetched. We know that they exist on the snouts of certain snakes, and this strengthens the case for their existence in dogs.

B Check the statements that the author would probably agree with.

1. ☑ Dogs have more kinds of sensory perceptions than people.
2. ☑ Scientists will probably be able to discover how dogs' senses work.
3. ☐ The behavior of wolves is irrelevant to the understanding of the behavior of dogs.
4. ☑ The behavior of some dogs during thunderstorms indicates that they are afraid of drowning.
5. ☑ The presence of heat detectors in some snakes proves that dogs have similar sensors.

Lesson A   Trends in reading

vocabulary

Correct the vocabulary mistakes by rewriting these sentences with one of the words or phrases in the box.

| crafts book | fiction | magazine | newspaper | tabloid |

1. Nonfiction books tell stories from the author's imagination.

   Fiction books tell stories from the author's imagination.

2. This comic book, like many others, presents the news in a sensational way.

   _____

3. If you want to learn how to knit or work with wood, you can buy a novel.

   _____

4. *Vogue* is a famous fashion tabloid with both beautiful photography and serious articles.

   _____

5. In many countries, there is a daily magazine that is considered to be the most authoritative in its presentation of the news.

   _____

grammar

Underline the sentence adverbs in these dialogs. Then write them in the chart below.

1. Jack: I don't trust the facts in this biography of Madonna.
    Lisa: Well, the author <u>clearly</u> did his research. Also, didn't he interview her extensively?
2. Martin: When is your book going to be published?
    Sophie: Apparently in November, but copies will be available to me in October.
3. Marc: I went to buy that new book on global warming, but I couldn't find it.
    Emma: Haven't you heard? It was removed from the bookstores. Supposedly, the author used material from other books without giving credit to the original authors.
4. Kurt: Did you read the book on van Gogh that was recently published?
    Teresa: Yes, I did. You will probably disagree, but I thought the writing was dull.
5. Josh: This is the third murder mystery I've read this month.
    Mark: Obviously you like that kind of book!
6. Etsuko: Robert Frost's poems seem to be about simple things. But a more careful reading unquestionably reveals deeper meaning.
    Julie: I didn't know you were such a Frost fan.

Certainty	Less certainty	Possibility
clearly		

3

grammar

Using sentence adverbs, rewrite these sentences to reflect your opinion. Then add a second sentence to explain your opinion.

1. Reading nonfiction is more educational than reading novels.

_____

_____

2. Young people today are not interested in reading newspapers.

_____

_____

3. There is a magazine available for almost any interest that a person might have.

_____

_____

4. Because of electronic publishing, books will disappear in the next 25 years.

_____

_____

5. The Internet is the most powerful communication medium since the printing press.

_____

_____

4

grammar

How does reading books and magazines compare with reading material on the Internet? Write five sentences using some of the sentence adverbs in the box.

apparently	obviously	probably	unfortunately
clearly	potentially	supposedly	unquestionably

1. _____

2. _____

3. _____

4. _____

5. _____

writing

A Choose either a magazine or a Web site that you are familiar with, and write a review of it. Your review should answer the following questions.

Magazines

1. What is the name of the magazine?
2. What kind of subject matter does the magazine contain?
3. Are the articles interesting and believable?
4. Does the magazine appeal to you visually?
5. Is the magazine worth the money?
6. Would you recommend the magazine to other people?

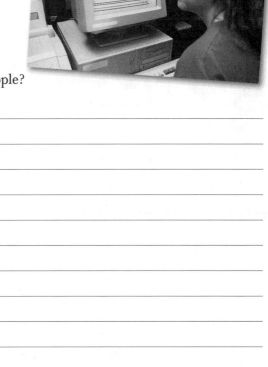

Web sites

1. What is the address of the Web site?
2. What is the general purpose of the Web site?
3. Can you trust the information on this Web site?
4. What visual or auditory features do you like or dislike on this Web site?
5. Technically, how well does the Web site work?
6. Would you recommend the Web site to other people?

_____

_____

_____

_____

_____

_____

_____

_____

_____

_____

_____

_____

B Reread your review. Are there places where adding sentence adverbs would make your writing better? If so, go back and add them.

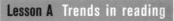

Lesson B *Television*

vocabulary

Match the phrases to make logical sentences.

1. Although most cartoon programs are designed to appeal to children, _d_

2. Quiz shows can be fun ____

3. Some people object to the violence ____

4. Talk shows can be very popular ____

5. Television viewers who like documentaries ____

6. The most popular television program this year is a sitcom ____

7. Viewers who enjoy watching love stories ____

a. are most likely to watch soap operas.

b. because they present real people talking about real-life experiences.

c. in which a family wins the lottery and moves into a mansion.

d. others are very sophisticated and appeal to adults.

e. tend to be people who want to learn new things.

f. that may occur on some drama series about law enforcement.

g. when you try to answer the questions faster than the participants do.

grammar

Rewrite these sentences. Place the negative adverb at the beginning of each sentence, and make other changes as necessary.

1. Television networks rarely showed movies in the early days of the medium.

   Rarely did television networks show movies in the early days of the medium.

2. Television seldom presents programs that challenge the viewer's intellect.

   _____

3. Television viewers will never lack choices in the future, mostly because of the continued popularity of satellite broadcasting.

   _____

4. These days, people in many parts of the world seldom go through a week without watching a movie on television.

   _____

5. Broadcasting in the United States never reflected the diversity of the population during its early years.

   _____

6. People living in remote areas can rarely get more than a few television channels unless they have cable.

   _____

7. Viewers have never had such a wide range of local programming.

   _____

3 Write six logical sentences by choosing one word or phrase from each column.

grammar

Television can be	addictive	you can find almost any kind of program that you want.
Soap operas are	absorbing to some children	I sent some money to her organization.
Nature documentaries are **such (a)**	diverse medium **that**	I watch as many of them as I can.
News programs can be	fascinating programs	they want to watch it all the time.
Television is **so**	inspirational	little information can be learned from them.
The documentary about Mother Teresa was	superficial	many people watch them every day.

1. _____

2. _____

3. _____

4. _____

5. _____

6. _____

4 Complete these sentences with opinions of your own.

grammar

1. Some drama series can be so _____*violent*_____ nowadays that _*I think children*_ _*shouldn't watch them.*_

2. Soap operas are so _____ that I _____
_____

3. _____ is such a great actor that I _____
_____

4. Commercials can be so _____ that I _____
_____

5. _____ is such a _____ that I laugh every
time I see it.

6. Watching television can be so _____ that I _____
_____

7. _____ is such a _____
program that I never watch it.

A   Read the article quickly to find the answers to these questions. Then read the article again carefully.

1. Who was Guglielmo Marconi? _____

2. Who invented television? _____

At Home, the TV Rules

In the late 1500s, a cannon was placed atop Signal Hill, in Newfoundland, to ward off invaders. Flags were also flown there to alert sailors to bad weather. It's fitting, then, that the Italian Guglielmo Marconi should have chosen this location to receive the world's first radio transmission – in Morse code – from England on December 12, 1901.

Marconi, combining earlier ideas with his own, ushered in a new communications era.

For the next 50 years, until the emergence of television, radio ruled the air waves.

Today, it's the TV that rules. No individual can claim to have invented television.

In 1884, the German Paul Nipkow invented a device that sent pictures mechanically, and in 1922, the American Phil Farnsworth invented an electronic scanning system. In 1906, Boris Rosing, a Russian, used a ray and a disc to create the world's first TV system. Then in the early 1920s, another Russian, Vladimir Zworykin, patented both the iconoscope, an electronic camera tube, and the kinescope, a picture display tube.

Shrewdly, Zworykin took out a patent for color TV, even though it wouldn't be developed for another 25 years.

In 1924, a Scot entered the scene – John Logie Baird. He first transmitted a moving silhouette image and a year later got the first actual TV picture.

In 1926, Baird successfully demonstrated TV in a London laboratory. Two years later in New York, Felix the Cat became the first TV star.

TV captured everyone's imagination, but hardly anyone had a set, with just two thousand in use worldwide in the mid-1930s.

Since the late 1940s, TV technology has jumped in leaps and bounds. Computers may eventually be combined with all televisions to give subscribers a total all-in-one communications network.

Today, it's possible to sit and watch a portable TV in the middle of the Amazon jungle or in the Arctic. It's amazing when one considers that Marconi was on Signal Hill in the same century.

B   Put the events in order.

____ the development of the first real TV system

____ the first transmission of a moving image

_1_ the invention of a device that sent pictures mechanically

____ Felix the Cat became the first TV star

____ the invention of a picture display tube

____ the invention of an electronic scanning system

C   Check the statements the writer would probably agree with.

1. ☐ Signal Hill was used historically as a site for communication.

2. ☐ Rarely do people listen to the radio nowadays.

3. ☐ Vladimir Zworykin was a very foolish man.

4. ☐ By the mid-1930s, television was the dominant medium of broadcasting.

5. ☐ The development of television was achieved quickly and by only two scientists.

6. ☐ Radio and television communication developed very rapidly in the twentieth century.

Lesson A *The enjoyment of art*

1

grammar

Choose the correct word to complete each sentence.

1. Generally, the more an artist is known, the _____*more*_____ money he or she makes. (more/less)

2. The _____ publicity an artist gets, the harder it is to make a living. (easier/less)

3. Some say that the _____ an artist is, the more he or she will develop artistically. (less/poorer)

4. The _____ a painting is shown in museums, the more famous it becomes. (longer/better)

5. In my opinion, the more you learn about some artists, the _____ you are able to understand them. (less/fewer)

6. For many collectors of modern art, the more shocking the subject, the _____. (sooner/better)

 2

grammar

Complete Lily's interview with the words from the box.

better	less	longer	more	sooner

Lily: How did you become an artist, Dante?

Dante: As a kid, I loved to draw. It seemed as though the more I drew, the _____ I got. By the time I was 10, I knew I wanted to be a painter.

Lily: Did you like to look at other artists' work?

Dante: I used to be a big fan of Andy Warhol, but the more I developed my own style, the _____ I felt he was my model. I then discovered that Jackson Pollock spoke most deeply to me.

Lily: But your style is nothing like Pollock's.

Dante: I know, but the more I studied his work, the _____ I learned that his sense of freedom was key. This freed me to create my own style.

Lily: Well, you've certainly succeeded in doing that. What's next for you, Dante?

Dante: The _____ I stay in New York, the more I realize I need a change. So I'm planning to spend some time in east Asia.

Lily: Why is that?

Dante: The art scene there is very exciting and dynamic.

Lily: Have you decided when you'll leave?

Dante: Not exactly, but I think the _____, the better.

3

vocabulary

Write the word that describes each art style in the blank. Then write a sentence that expresses your own opinion about each style.

cubism	impressionism	pop art	surrealism

1. _____

2. _____

3. _____

4. _____

4

grammar

Rewrite these sentences to make them true for you. If the sentence is already true for you, write a sentence to support your opinion.

1. The more contemporary art I see, the more I like it.

_____

2. The more unusual an artist is, the less interested I become in his or her work.

_____

3. The more artists show reality in paintings, the more likely I am to enjoy it.

_____

4. The more a government tries to support art, the worse a country's art inevitably becomes.

_____

5. The more time children spend learning about art, the less they will learn about more important things.

_____

writing

A Read the thesis statements. Do the topics belong in the composition? Check yes (**Y**) or no (**N**).

1. Thesis statement: Artists should receive financial support to help them get started in their careers.

	Y	N
a. Artists can get money from government programs.	☐	☐
b. Artists can save money by living less expensively.	☐	☐
c. Artists can apply for money from foundations that support the arts.	☐	☐
d. Artists can participate in residence programs at universities, giving them time to teach for money.	☐	☐

2. Thesis statement: African art is as diverse as the continent itself, but the exhibit at the Art Africa Gallery offers a collection of pieces that represents this diversity quite well.

	Y	N
a. the mask art of the Dogon of Mali, in West Africa	☐	☐
b. the architectural art of the Tambera people of Togo, in West Africa	☐	☐
c. the beaded jewelry of the Masai of Kenya, in East Africa	☐	☐
d. the influence of African art on European art	☐	☐

3. Thesis statement: Architects of the early twentieth century radically changed the way Americans built houses and office buildings.

	Y	N
a. Henry Louis Sullivan was an innovator in skyscraper design.	☐	☐
b. Frank Lloyd Wright changed the way Americans think about house design.	☐	☐
c. Stanford White originated the "shingle-style" house, which became a distinctive kind of American dwelling.	☐	☐
d. Philip Johnson had a great impact on the design of office buildings in the 1970s and 1980s.	☐	☐

4. Thesis statement: The new exhibit at the Metropolitan Museum of Painting offers an excellent overview of the three main painting styles in France from the end of the nineteenth century to the beginning of the twentieth century.

	Y	N
a. an exhibit on impressionism, represented by painters such as Renoir, Degas, and Monet	☐	☐
b. an exhibit on expressionism, represented by painters such as van Gogh and Gauguin	☐	☐
c. an exhibit on sculptors such as Rodin	☐	☐
d. an exhibit on cubism, represented by painters such as Picasso and Braque	☐	☐

B How would you choose to classify the art in your culture? Write a thesis statement and three topics.

The importance of music

vocabulary

Write two sentences describing each type of music, choosing from the words in the box. Some words may be used more than once.

African-American origins	soft	uses drums
based on music of cowboys	soothing	uses electric instruments
improvisation	strong beat	uses simple instruments
instrumental	strong rhythm	uses stringed instruments
popular in southern U.S.	traditional	

1. country and western *Country and western music, based on the music of cowboys, uses stringed instruments. It's especially popular in the southern United States.*

2. folk *Folk music based on African-American origins uses drums*

3. jazz *Jazz based on improvisation of strong beats uses simple instrument*

4. new age *new age based on instrumental uses stringed instruments & strong rhythm*

5. rock 'n' roll *Rock 'n' roll based on popular in southern music U.S.*

grammar

Check the sentences that have mistakes. Then rewrite them in another way.

1. ☑ Knowing how much you like jazz, this Louis Armstrong CD will please you.

   Knowing how much you like jazz, I got this Louis Armstrong CD for you.

2. ☑ Having listened to the Beatles growing up, Marian decided to visit their hometown of Liverpool.

   _____

3. ☐ Being very young, everyone was astonished by Mozart.

   _____

4. ☐ Liking Ricky Martin as I do, these concert tickets mean a lot to me.

   _____

5. ☐ Having started her career at an early age, the violinist Midori was famous by the time she was a teenager.

   _____

6. ☑ Having performed all over the world, New York is the pianist's favorite city.

   I think New york is the pianist's favorite city.

3 Rewrite these sentences using participial phrases.

grammar

1. Because they started the concert with their hit song, the band got the audience on their feet.

   Having started the concert with their hit song, the band got the audience on their feet.

2. Since he knew his solo was coming up, the guitarist stepped to the front of the stage.

   Knowing his solo was coming up, the guitarist stepped to the front of the stage.

3. As they pushed up against the stage, some fans then tried to climb onto it.

   Pushing up against the stage, some fans (then) tried to climb onto it.

4. Because he looked down at the right time, the guitarist was able to avoid falling over the fans.

   Having looked down at the right time, the guitarist was able to avoid falling over the fans.

5. As they thought this was a dangerous situation, the guards made fans step back from the stage.

   Thinking that this was a dangerous situation, the guards made fans step back from the stage.

6. Since they realized that the guards had averted a potentially dangerous situation, the band publicly thanked them.

   turn aside

   Realizing that the guards have averted a potentially dangerous situation, the band publicly thanked them

4 Reduce these clauses to participial phrases. Then complete the sentences.

grammar

1. As I listened to different kinds of music growing up,

   Having listened to different kinds of music growing up, I

2. Because Elvis Presley sold so many records worldwide,

   Having sold so many records worldwide, Elvis...

3. Because teenagers know that parents may not like loud music,

   Knowing that parents may not like loud music

4. Since rock 'n' roll music has such an appeal to young people,

   Having such an appeal to young people rock 'n' roll...

5. Since music producers realize that videos are so appealing,

   Realizing

A Read the article. What do you think the root *neuro* means?

Music May Someday Help Repair the Brain

The music that makes the foot tap, the fingers snap, and the pulse quicken stirs the brain at its most fundamental levels, suggesting that scientists one day may be able to retune damaged minds by exploiting rhythm, harmony, and melody, according to new research.

"Undeniably, there is a biology of music," said Harvard University Medical School neurobiologist Mark Jude Tramo. "Music is biologically part of human life, just as music is aesthetically part of human life."

Researchers found that the brain:

• Responds directly to harmony. Neuroscientists discovered that different parts of the brain involved in emotion are activated depending on whether the music is pleasant or unpleasant.

• Interprets written music in an area on the brain's right side. That region corresponds to an area on the opposite side of the brain known to handle written words and letters. So, researchers uncovered an anatomical link between music and language.

• Grows in response to musical training. In a study of classically trained musicians, researchers discovered that male musicians have significantly larger brains than men who have not had extensive musical training.

Overall, music seems to involve the brain at almost every level, and researchers are already looking for ways to harness the power of music to change the brain. Preliminary research also suggests that music may play some role in enhancing intelligence. Indeed, so seductive is the possibility that music can boost a child's IQ that some politicians are lobbying for schoolchildren to be exposed regularly to Mozart sonatas, although such research has yet to be confirmed.

The scientists said the new research could help the clinical practice of neurology, including cognitive rehabilitation. As a therapeutic tool, for example, some doctors already use music to help rehabilitate stroke patients. Surprisingly, some stroke patients who have lost their ability to speak retain their ability to sing, and that opens an avenue for therapists to retrain the brain's speech centers.

B Read these statements. Are they supported by the research? Check yes (**Y**) or no (**N**).

	Y	N
1. Different areas of the brain respond to music.	☐	☐
2. The brains of classically trained male musicians grow larger than the brains of nonmusician males.	☐	☐
3. The brains of classically trained female musicians do not grow larger than nonmusician females.	☐	☐
4. Children who listen to Mozart sonatas develop higher intelligence than those who do not have exposure to this music.	☐	☐
5. Some stroke victims who are unable to speak are able to sing.	☐	☐

Lesson A   *Lifestyles in transition*

grammar

Underline the relative pronouns in this announcement.

If these statements describe your situation, then telecommuting may be right for you.

1. You have a job <u>that</u> you can do independently of your co-workers.
2. You can work productively without the pressure <u>that you may get</u> from supervisors.
3. Your home has a quiet room <u>which you</u> can use as your office.
4. You have the office equipment <u>that you</u> will need to do your job at home.
5. There are no family members <u>who will</u> bother you while you are trying to work.
6. You won't miss the social interaction <u>that many people enjoy</u>.
7. The people <u>who you deal with</u> outside the company will have no problems with your telecommuting.
8. You can effectively use the telephone and E-mail to communicate with co-workers <u>whose help you may</u> need while you are away from the office.

See your Human Resources representative for details of our telecommuting policy.

grammar

Combine these sentences using a defining relative clause.

1. Keeping physically fit is an important goal. A lot of people try to achieve this goal these days.

   Keeping physically fit is an important goal that a lot of people try to achieve these days.

2. Many people stay fit. These people find the time to work out regularly at a gym.

3. For best results, it's important to find a gym. You like this gym.

4. It may be a good idea to hire a trainer. A trainer can work with you privately.

5. Your trainer can give you exercise advice. The advice can help you avoid injuries.

6. If you get bored at the gym, try bringing a CD player. You can listen to this player while you exercise.

7. To help with motivation, work out with a "gym pal." You enjoy the gym pal's company.

8. Concentrate on the parts of your body. These parts of your body need the most work.

3

grammar

Use defining relative clauses and information of your own to complete these sentences.

1. I have always admired people _who/that_ _____

_____

2. I've always thought that I would enjoy a lifestyle _that_ _____

_____

3. Mothers _who_ _____

_____ should be greatly admired.

4. These days many people want jobs _that_ _____

_____

5. Finding enough time to spend with family and friends is a problem _____

_____

6. In my opinion, medical therapies _____

_____ should be emphasized in health care.

4

vocabulary

Complete these conversations with words or phrases from the box.

| alternative medicine | fitness | telecommuting | voluntary simplicity |
| bodybuilding | homeschooling | vegetarianism | |

1. A: I see your car at the gym every morning at 7:00. You must care a lot about _____ _fitness_ _____.
   B: Well, I do, but it's more than that. I'm taking a class in _bodybuilding_ _____. I want to start participating in weight-lifting competitions next year.

2. A: Did you give up meat for ethical reasons?
   B: No, _vegetarianism_ _____ simply provides me with a much healthier diet.

3. A: Is Craig in the office today? I need to ask him about these numbers.
   B: This is his day for _telecommuting_ _____, but you can reach him at home.

4. A: I don't understand why Kazuko drives that old car. She could certainly afford something better.
   B: She doesn't like to spend money on unnecessary things because she practices _voluntary simplicity_.

5. A: Which school do your kids attend?
   B: Oh, we don't send them to school. We do _homeschooling_ _____ because we find they do better in that environment.

6. A: My doctor has prescribed pills to control my allergies, but I don't like the idea of putting so many chemicals into my body.
   B: You should look into _alternative med_ _____ instead. Some of those remedies may help you.

A Read this composition and answer the questions.

I feel it is very important for families to have regular meals together. One of my most positive childhood memories was dinner with my parents and two sisters. As a result, last year I decided that the entire family would have dinner together three days a week. Because my husband and I both work and our three kids are busy with school activities, we found that we rarely had a chance to get together as a family. But we thought it would be possible for everyone to set aside three evenings a week for a sit-down dinner.

First we tried setting three fixed days for our experiment – Mondays, Wednesdays, and Fridays. After a couple of weeks of trying this plan, almost everyone was unhappy. Then my son had the idea of having everyone post his or her schedule for the week on the refrigerator every Sunday. I would choose the three best days, and those with scheduling conflicts. . . .

For a while, the kids continued to resist the idea. They said they would rather spend the time with their friends or participating in sports or other activities. Gradually, though, they began to see these evenings together in a very positive way. We laughed a lot. We made plans for trips. We discussed each other's problems. After a couple of months, anyone who had to miss a family meal felt. . . .

We all feel that we have been able to build much stronger relationships within the family than we had before. Of course, there are still disagreements, jealousies, and rivalries, but we communicate better with each other now. The idea of having regular family meals together, which seemed difficult at first, has brought about many positive changes in our lives.

1. What is the thesis statement?

_____

2. What is the focus of the second paragraph?

It focus on how scheduling days of the week to get together ↙

3. What is the focus of the third paragraph?

It focus on how gradually people start enjoying these evenings reunions.

4. What sentence in the conclusion restates the thesis statement?

The idea of having regular family meals together which seems difficult at first has brought about many positive changes

B Write a thesis statement for a composition about an important decision you have made recently.

_____

_____

_____

C Now write your composition. Include two paragraphs providing background information and details, and a conclusion.

Lesson B — Setting goals

1

grammar

Choose the correct expression to complete these sentences.

1. I often feel _____as though_____ I'm losing touch with some of my old high school friends.   (as/as though)

2. Traveling on business doesn't bother me _____ it did when the weather was colder.   (as/as if)

3. Paul is such a perfectionist that he acts _____ nothing is ever good enough.   (as/as if)

4. I feel _____ I've accomplished a lot of the goals I set for myself when I was younger.   (as/like)

5. Making a lot of money in my career doesn't concern me _____ it did when I first started working.   (as if/the way)

6. I really admire Charlotte because she acts _____ she can do anything in this world.   (as though/the way)

7. Someday I hope to be able to retire early _____ my father did.   (as if/like)

2

grammar

Match the phrases to make logical sentences. Then rewrite the sentences to make them more formal.

1. Many women workers feel _e_

2. Planning early for retirement doesn't concern young people ____

3. If you want to lose weight, you don't have to work out ____

4. Not knowing what the future will bring doesn't bother me ____

5. I know I need to save more money because sometimes I spend ____

6. Getting involved in community activities helps new arrivals to a city feel ____

a. like I'm a millionaire.

b. like you are a bodybuilder, but you should get plenty of exercise.

c. like it did when I was younger.

d. like they belong there.

e. like they can't advance in their jobs as quickly as men can.

f. like it does older people.

1. _Many women workers feel as if they can't advance in their jobs as quickly as men can._

2. _____

3. _____

4. _____

5. _____

6. _____

3 Read each situation and answer the questions using *as if*, *as though*, or *like*.

grammar

1. Bill has tried everything in order to lose weight and hasn't seen any results. How does he feel?

   He feels as though nothing has worked.
   _____

2. Marjorie has been under a lot of pressure recently and hasn't had a break from work for months. How does she feel?

   _____
   _____

3. Kenzo is trying to take on more responsibility at home, but today is a busy day. How does he feel?

   _____
   _____

4. Lucinda has gained a lot of confidence in her ability to use English, and she isn't afraid to make mistakes. How does she feel?

   _____
   _____

4 Complete these sentences so that they are true for you.

grammar

1. I feel as though I don't have enough money to _____
   _____

2. I don't _____
   _____ the way I did when I was younger.

3. Nowadays I think many people act as if they _____
   _____

4. I still _____
   _____ just as I did last year.

5. I feel like I need _____
   _____

5

A Read this article. Find the underlined words and phrases that match these definitions.

1. a 100-year-old person _____centenarian_____
2. remove _____
3. mentally ill _____
4. very quick mentally _____
5. of advanced years _____

Centenarian Planning

If you thought retirement planning is hard, wait until you get a glimpse of "**centenarian** planning." You'd better pull up a rocking chair.

It has been predicted that millions of people currently 50 and older will make it to the age of 100, says neuropsychologist Margery H. Silver, associate director of the New England Centenarian Study. "It has also been predicted that every female child born today has a 50-50 chance of living to be a hundred," she says.

An instructor in psychology at the Harvard Medical School, Silver says one conclusion to emerge from the study of centenarians in the Boston area is that if you are going to live to be a hundred, you have to plan to live a healthy and forward-looking lifestyle. Not only will that help you reach a **ripe** old age, it will make living to a hundred more worthwhile if you do.

One of Silver's findings in the study is that a quarter of its 100 or so centenarians were "cognitively intact," and another substantial number "were thinking quite well," she says. "That went against the common thinking that by the time you get to be a hundred everyone will be **demented**."

The lesson from those who were **sharp as a tack** at age one hundred? "Keep mentally active," says Silver, recounting how one of her centenarians, at 104, learned an entirely new branch of mathematics and started writing articles about it. "Exercising your brain is as important as exercising your body," she says.

As for physical well-being, Silver acknowledges that some people have the genetic edge in reaching 100 — but lifestyle choices count for a lot. "Most of us have the genetic factor to live well into our eighties," says Silver, "so we really need to pay attention to taking good care of our health."

Making preventive health choices in our lives early on — such as not smoking, avoiding saturated fats, drinking only moderately, keeping trim, avoiding too much sun, exercising, and taking the right vitamins — can add 10 or more quality years to anyone's life, explains Silver. Of course, not doing those things can **subtract** years.

B Check the advice that the article mentions.

1. ☐ Avoid habits that lead to bad health, such as smoking.
2. ☐ Do things to keep your mind active.
3. ☐ Get lots of sun as often as possible.
4. ☐ Practice physical fitness.
5. ☐ Get an annual checkup from your doctor.
6. ☐ Avoid vitamins.

Lesson A *What's new on the market?*

Underline the direct objects and circle the indirect objects in each sentence.

grammar

1. Today's computers give their users many more options than before.
2. Advertising is useful because it tells us news about improved products.
3. The salesman recommended the new software to me.
4. Someone had to explain the new printer to Daniel.
5. This palm-top computer must have cost you a lot of money.
6. You should mail this card to the company for a rebate.
7. I don't shop on-line because I like to ask salespeople questions in person.

Unscramble the words and phrases to make correct sentences.

grammar

1. the latest computers/showed/the woman/the salesclerk

   The salesclerk showed the woman the latest computers.

2. the woman/to/the PX-2000/recommended/the salesclerk

   _____

3. her/the main features/he/described/to

   _____

4. him/the woman/the price/asked

   _____

5. the clerk/$2,500/her/told

   _____

6. nothing/said/to/him/she/for a moment

   _____

7. a discount/offered/the clerk/her

   _____

8. the money/the clerk/she/to/gave

   _____

43

Use the words in the box to give advice about what to do in each situation.

grammar

| lend | mention | recommend | return | teach |

1. Vickie got a classical music CD from her brother for her birthday, but she prefers rock 'n' roll.
   Vickie should _____

2. Ben and Pam want to go skiing with Sue this weekend, but Pam doesn't have enough money.
   _____

3. Glen is a computer programmer. His sister wants to buy a computer, but she doesn't know much about them.
   _____

4. Robin's favorite Italian restaurant is Luigi's. Her father wants to eat Italian food but doesn't know any restaurants.
   _____

5. Max sold his car to a neighbor. The car uses a lot of oil, but he forgot to say anything about it. His neighbor is going to take a long trip.
   _____

Write a sentence about each situation using the words in the box.

vocabulary

| bargain hunter | compulsive shopper | shopping spree |
| black market | price war | window-shopping |

1. Monika and Emi love to go to shopping districts and look at what's on sale. They can spend hours doing this, without buying anything at all!
   _____

2. When Sam gets paid, he always stops by the mall on the way home to buy things for himself, whether he needs them or not. He will sometimes spend all of his money in one day.
   _____

3. Mark never pays the full price for anything. No matter what he needs, he will shop around for the best price. He will even go to a different part of the city in search of a good price.
   _____

4. Before her wedding, Anne and her mother spent a week shopping for everything they would need for the wedding and for Anne's new home. They spent a lot and had a great time.
   _____

5. In the United States, Cuban cigars cannot be imported because of government regulations. However, if you really want a Cuban cigar, you can usually find one, despite the legal restrictions.
   _____

6. Big computer manufacturers and retail stores keep cutting their prices to attract new customers. Some companies are even willing to lose money in order to gain new customers.
   _____

writing

A For each opinion, check the two supporting examples and details that support it. Then write another sentence to support the opinion.

1. Today's children are too materialistic.

   a. ☐ Many children have more free time than they have ever had before.

   b. ☐ They compete to have the "coolest" clothes and the most expensive hobbies.

   c. ☐ Parents complain that children only want money from them.

   _____

   _____

   _____

2. Digital cameras are superior to traditional cameras.

   a. ☐ Digital cameras don't require film, so in the long run they are cheaper.

   b. ☐ A good traditional camera costs about the same as a good digital camera.

   c. ☐ Pictures from digital cameras can be used on the Internet without scanning.

   _____

   _____

   _____

3. Talking on a cell phone while driving is dangerous.

   a. ☐ In case of an accident, a driver can call the police on the cell phone.

   b. ☐ Police say that many accidents happen while a driver is talking on a cell phone.

   c. ☐ Drivers don't pay attention to traffic when they are talking on a cell phone.

   _____

   _____

   _____

B Write a thesis statement about one of the opinions above or one of your own.

_____

_____

C Write a composition. Include your thesis statement in the first paragraph, and develop your opinion with examples and details in subsequent paragraphs.

Lesson B *Consumer beware*

grammar

1 Maria has asked her father for advice because she has accumulated so much credit card debt. Underline the subjunctive verbs in his response.

> Maria,
>   I'm sorry that you are in this situation, and I know it's not easy to get out of debt. If you're serious about it, it's essential that you <u>make</u> some changes in your lifestyle and spending habits. Here's what I suggest that you do. First, I strongly recommend that you start working full-time instead of part-time, and I propose that all of your extra money go toward the credit card debt. Second, I advise that you cut your expenses by 25%. It is crucial for you to spend money only on essential things for a while. Third, I think it's imperative that you sell your car. I suggest you take the bus to work until you can afford a car. I think that if you do these things, you will be in a much better position in about a year.
>   Let me know how you're doing. Good luck!
> Love, Dad

grammar

2 Rewrite each sentence in another way without changing the meaning.

1. It is necessary that people be on the lookout for consumer fraud.

   It is necessary for people to be on the lookout for consumer fraud.

2. It is important that you keep your receipts for all major purchases.

   _____

3. It is essential for people to purchase only what they can afford.

   _____

4. It is vital that consumers read the labels when purchasing medicine.

   _____

5. It is imperative for retailers to be aware of their main competitors.

   _____

grammar

3 Complete these sentences with ideas of your own.

1. If you want to get the best electronics prices, I suggest that _____

   _____

2. If you buy something that you later realize doesn't fit, I recommend that _____

   _____

3. If you think that you are a compulsive shopper, it is important that _____

   _____

4. If you dislike shopping in large stores, I propose that _____

   _____

vocabulary

What type of advertising would you use for each product? Write a sentence under each picture explaining your choice.

airplane banner	flyers	Internet banner	telemarketing
billboard	full-page ad	radio commercial	TV commercial

1. ice cream *I would use an airplane banner because everyone could see it, and many people might want something to eat.*

2. investment services _____

3. men's suits _____

4. discount books _____

5. car wash _____

6. computer games _____

A Read the article. What do you think? Is a "shop-till-you-drop" habit comparable to binge eating?

Behavior Study on Shopaholics

Compulsive shoppers may have a new psychological excuse to blame for their wild shopping sprees. Psychologists at the University of Canterbury in New Zealand are investigating the "shop-till-you-drop" habit as a behavioral disorder comparable to binge eating. The symptoms are that shoppers frequently buy more than they can afford or more than they need, and it causes them distress.

"It becomes a problem when you are out of control," senior psychology lecturer Neville Blampied said. "When you are feeling bad and blue, what do you do? Some people eat chocolate cake and half a quart of ice cream. Some people take the credit card and go out to the mall.

"Bank managers are aware of the problem because they have to deal with people who have to be ceremoniously stripped of their credit cards."

Compulsive shopping was first identified in 1915, although it was then known as oniomania. Few studies have been done on the problem.

An advertisement in a suburban Christchurch paper, calling for volunteers to participate in an experimental treatment program codesigned by Mr. Blampied, attracted 10 replies. But the problem, said Mr. Blampied, is "clearly not rare."

He is concerned that compulsive shopping tends to fall into the realm of psychiatry and is treated with drugs. "As psychologists we are interested in nondrug treatments for behavioral difficulties," Mr. Blampied said.

Compulsive eaters or shoppers get a kick from their habit. "Both activities provide an immediate kind of arousal and a bit of a boost and you feel a bit better," he said. "You have long-term problems in consequence, but human beings are extremely good at discounting long-term problems and are hypersensitive to short-term benefits," he said.

The therapy's aim was to help people find better ways of managing their negative emotions. The program, consisting of 10 one-hour weekly sessions and two follow-up treatments, is loosely based on teaching stress management.

"You often have to start to get people to correctly recognize their emotions. Not being able to discriminate what you really feel impairs your ability to solve the problems associated with what's making you feel that way," Mr. Blampied said.

B Check the correct answer for each question.

1. What is this article mostly about?
   a. ☐ the warning signs of compulsive shopping
   b. ☐ effective treatments for compulsive shopping
   c. ☐ how compulsive shopping is like compulsive eating

2. When might people indulge in compulsive shopping?
   a. ☐ when they have lots of money
   b. ☐ when they are feeling sad
   c. ☐ when they are taking drugs

3. Which is considered to be important in therapy for compulsive shoppers?
   a. ☐ teaching them to manage their money better
   b. ☐ teaching them to understand their emotions
   c. ☐ treating them with drugs

Lesson A

A wild bunch!

Complete the sentences with *whoever* or *whatever*.

grammar

1. Fossils are fascinating to _____ wants to learn about early life on earth.

2. _____ visits a display of dinosaur fossils at a museum will be amazed by the size of these creatures.

3. Paleontologists search constantly for _____ helps them understand how these animals lived.

4. _____ studies dinosaurs must wonder why they became extinct.

5. According to some scientists, _____ killed the dinosaurs could happen again in modern times.

6. _____ doubts that animal species can become extinct should learn about what happened to the dinosaurs.

Read this paragraph about bats. Then rewrite the numbered sentences using *whoever* or *whatever*.

grammar

> ⌐1⌐ Anyone who thinks that bats are dangerous pests is wrong in most cases. In fact, most species of bats are helpful to human beings. Sixty to seventy percent of bat species eat insects. ⌐2⌐ These bats will eat anything that they find as they fly through the air at night. Some people even try to attract bats to their property to help control mosquitoes. Other bats are necessary to the pollination of specific species of plants. ⌐3⌐ Unfortunately, bats are frightening to everyone who believes in the old stories of vampire bats. In reality, only three species of bats feed on blood, usually only from small animals. It is true, however, that vampire bats can spread diseases such as rabies to other species. Even though many people will continue to dislike and fear bats, it is important to remember that they are an important part of the ecology, especially in rain forests. ⌐4⌐ Anything that endangers bats in these areas will also affect the regions' fragile ecosystems. ⌐5⌐ Anyone who is interested in learning more about bats can visit his or her local library.

1. _____

2. _____

3. _____

4. _____

5. _____

grammar

Do you agree with these statements? Respond to what the first speaker says. Write sentences with *whoever* or *whatever*.

1. A: Anyone who sees an injured wild animal should pick it up immediately and take it to a veterinarian.

   B: *I disagree. Whoever sees an injured animal should leave it alone.*

2. A: We should admire everybody who fights for the rights of endangered animals.

   B: _____

   _____

3. A: Governments should stop anything that threatens an endangered animal's habitat.

   B: _____

   _____

4. A: Any person who claims not to be afraid of snakes or rodents is lying.

   B: _____

   _____

5. A: Anything that is considered dangerous, such as a wolf or a shark, should not be given the same amount of protection as other animals.

   B: _____

   _____

vocabulary

Complete these sentences with the words from the box.

amphibians	mammals	primates	reptiles	rodents

1. According to evolutionary theory, _____, which include primates and rodents, appeared much later than reptiles.

2. Because _____ must chew tough vegetable material to survive, they have evolved a way of keeping their front teeth sharp.

3. Most _____ communicate with each other in complex ways, including gestures, facial expressions, and vocal interchange.

4. Because they can live on land or water, _____ are often very adaptable animals.

5. _____ are cold-blooded; therefore, they can't live in the polar regions.

writing

A Read the two positions about dams. Then find the supporting reasons for each position, and write them in the blanks.

Positions

1. Dams are harmful and should be torn down.

   _____

   _____

   _____

2. Dams benefit people and should be maintained.

   _____

   _____

   _____

> **Reasons**
> - Dams provide water for the irrigation of crops.
> - Dams permanently alter the ecosystem of rivers.
> - Dams provide recreational and sporting opportunities.
> - Dams provide much-needed electricity.
> - Dams prevent fish from migrating to their breeding grounds.
> - Dams encourage pollution because of housing developments along the shore.

B Which position is closest to your opinion? Write the first paragraph of a persuasive composition to explain your point of view. Then write the remaining paragraphs of your composition on a separate sheet of paper. Be sure to argue against the opposing view.

_____

_____

_____

_____

_____

_____

_____

Lesson B *"Man's best friend"*

grammar

Complete these sentences using *whenever* or *wherever*. If the time or place is specified, use *when* or *where*.

1. For some reason, _____ I go with my pet rat, someone gets upset.

2. Owners of reptiles have to be careful _____ they keep their cages. Reptiles are cold-blooded and will not survive if they are exposed to cold weather.

3. Research indicates that _____ a person strokes animals, his or her blood pressure goes down. Also, it's been argued that trained dogs should be present _____ there are people recovering from illnesses.

4. _____ I got home last night, I took my two dogs out for a long walk. They are always so eager to be with me. _____ I go, they are delighted to follow me.

5. _____ I adopted my dog, I took on a serious responsibility. Being able to keep a pet healthy and happy depends on your lifestyle – _____ you live.

grammar

Rewrite the last sentence of each dialog with a sentence including a clause starting with *whenever* or *wherever*.

1. A: I'm going over to Nancy's apartment. Would you like to come with me?

   B: No, I can't. She has a cat, and I'm allergic to them. Every time I'm around a cat, I start sneezing.

   Whenever I'm around a cat, I start sneezing.

2. A: Did you enjoy your walk in the park?

   B: Yes, but it wasn't like in my city. No matter where I went, there were dogs running around without their owners.

   _____

3. A: What's wrong with your cat? She looks upset.

   B: She's just excited. She looks like that every time she sees a bird outside.

   _____

4. A: I'm happy to take care of your bird while you're gone. How often does he need to be fed?

   B: Some days he eats a lot, but some days he doesn't. Just put more food in his dish when you notice that it's empty.

   _____

5. A: What kind of pet would you like to have?

   B: Well, I love fish. Every time I watch fish swimming, I feel calm, no matter where I am.

   _____

grammar

Read these situations and answer the questions. Use clauses with *whenever* or *wherever*.

1. Patty's neighbor has a huge dog. She can't tell if the man is walking the dog or the other way around. How does Patty react when she sees them?

_____

_____

2. Joon thinks that horses are the most beautiful and graceful animals on earth. How does he feel when he sees one running across a field?

_____

_____

3. Beth is interested in reptiles and enjoys studying them in her spare time. What does she do every time she takes a vacation?

_____

_____

4. Ray has a turkey named Winnie, who hates to be alone. She goes with him to the store, to the bank – all over. Where does Winnie go?

_____

_____

4

grammar

Combine the phrases from the two columns to make logical sentences.

Whenever I see a puppy,	they have no time to care for them.
Pet reptiles should be kept where	it chooses to go.
People shouldn't have pets when	there is sunlight and fresh air.
A caged bird cannot fly wherever	I want to get one.

1. _____

2. _____

3. _____

4. _____

A Read the title and first paragraph of this story, and answer these questions. Then read the rest of the story.

1. Do you think the people in the story will have good or bad luck? _____
2. Do you think that this will be a true story? _____

A Fairy Tale Comes True

Every Bosnian child knows the story of a poor woman who caught a golden fish, released it, and in return gained wealth and happiness. It's a Balkan fairy tale – but it turned into reality for one poor family.

"What happened here is beyond good luck – it really is a fable," said Admir Malkoc.

In 1990, Smajo Malkoc returned from working in Austria to Jezero, a village surrounding a lake, in the former Yugoslavia. He had an unusual gift for his teenaged sons, Dzevad and Catib: an aquarium with two goldfish.

Two years passed. War broke out. As Bosnian Serb forces advanced on Jezero, the women and children fled. Bosnian Muslim men tried to resist. Smajo Malkoc was killed.

When his wife, Fehima, sneaked back into the destroyed village to bury her husband, she spotted the fish in the aquarium. She let them out into the nearby lake. "This way they might be more fortunate than us," she recalls thinking.

Fast-forward to 1995. Fehima returned with her sons to Jezero to find ruins. Eyes misting over, she turned toward the lake and glimpsed something strange. She came closer – and caught her breath.

"The whole lake was shining from the golden fish in it," she said. During the years of war and killing all around the lake, life underwater had flourished.

After their return, Fehima and her sons started feeding the fish and then selling them. Now, homes, bars, and coffee shops in the region have aquariums containing fish from Jezero.

The Malkoc house, rebuilt from ruins, is one of the biggest in the village. The family says it has enough money not to have to worry about the future.

Other residents are welcome to catch and sell the fish. But most leave that to the Malkocs. "They threw the fish into the lake," said a villager. "It's their miracle."

B Put the events in order.

____ Mrs. Malkoc put the fish in a lake.

____ The war broke out.

____ The Malkoc family began caring for and feeding the fish in the lake.

____ The Malkocs rebuilt their house.

____ Mrs. Malkoc and the children returned to their home.

____ Mr. Malkoc was killed.

____ The Malkoc family began selling the fish.

____ Mrs. Malkoc returned to the village.

_1_ Smajo Malkoc brought two goldfish home for his children.

Lesson A · The nature of language

grammar

Underline the correct form of the verbs in this paragraph.

Some experts in communication **was/were** asked about E-mail and how it is being used today. They say that everyone who **uses/use** E-mail realizes that a special style has evolved for this medium. While some writers of E-mail write in a formal style, the majority **chooses/choose** a very informal style. In fact, a lot of informal messages **is/are** almost conversational in style. E-mail messages may also include abbreviations that not everyone **understands/understand**. A lot of younger users **tends/tend** to write with abbreviations such as *btw* for *by the way*. Only a minority of E-mail writers **includes/include** customary formulas such as *Dear Mr. Smith* and *Sincerely yours.* None of the experts **feels/feel** that a very informal style is appropriate for business E-mail messages.

grammar

Read these results from a student survey. Then use the words in the box to make statements. Use each word only once.

Why do you study a foreign language?

	Percentage of students
1. I expect to get a better job.	65%
2. I want to use the language for travel.	100%
3. I have to because it's a required subject.	30%
4. I need to be able to read the literature of the language.	0%
5. I do it just for fun.	50%

all	half	majority	minority	none

1. want to use the language for travel

_____

2. do it just for fun

_____

3. expect to get a better job

_____

4. need to be able to read the literature of the language

_____

5. have to because it's a required subject

_____

3

grammar

Complete these sentences with your own ideas.

1. Each language in the world is _____

_____

2. A lot of English vocabulary is _____

_____

3. All bilingual people use _____

_____

4. The majority of older people speak _____

_____

5. Every one of my classmates _____

_____

6. The majority of TV newscasters _____

_____

4

vocabulary

Complete the dialogs by using one of the expressions in the box. Make any changes as necessary.

> get a word in edgewise
> have a sharp tongue
> have a way with words
> love to hear oneself talk
> stick to the point
> talk behind one's back
> talk one into anything

1. A: Ms. Kang read my report and said some awful things about it.
   B: Well, she _____ , but she's also very
      perceptive. Just try to focus on what she's saying about your work.
2. A: Did Peter say anything about me after I left?
   B: Of course not. Peter would never _____ .
      He'd tell you directly.
3. A: Did you tell Lisa about our plans for her birthday?
   B: I tried to, but she kept talking about her problems with her car. I couldn't

   _____ .

4. A: I really liked what Mr. Ortega said about everyone working together as a team.
   B: I agree. It was very inspiring. He really _____ .
5. A: I know you want to talk about this report, but I'd like to tell you about my new customer.
   B: Let's _____ . We can talk about that later.
6. A: That meeting lasted so long! Al went on and on. No one could get a word in edgewise.
   B: He sure _____ , doesn't he?
7. A: Are you going to the company picnic this weekend?
   B: I was planning to work in my garden instead, but May convinced me to go. She certainly
      can _____ !

writing

A Read this passage. Underline the information that would belong in a summary.

English has had a long tradition of borrowing words from other languages. This tradition began with the conquest of Britain by the Norman-French in 1066. Because these conquerors established themselves as rulers, their dialect of French became the language of the aristocracy, of government, and of education. During this period, many French words came into the English language. Another strong influx of vocabulary came from Latin, which was the language of the church. Today, those words derived from French and Latin, though still identifiable as such, are an inseparable part of the English vocabulary and are not thought of as foreign by English speakers. In fact, the first two sentences of this paragraph contain three words that come to us from this tradition: *tradition*, *languages*, and *conquest*.

The British colonial era, which began with outposts in North America in the early seventeenth century, brought English speakers into contact with many other languages. In North America, words from the Native American peoples quickly found their way into the language. Examples include *moccasin* (a kind of soft shoe), *squash* (a vegetable), and *succotash* (a dish made with corn and squash).

The presence of Spanish colonies in North America led to the adoption of numerous Spanish words, such as *siesta* (a nap) and *tortilla* (a flat thin pancake made of wheat or corn flour). Asian languages also made contributions. For example, the word *pajamas* comes from a Hindi word, *khaki* comes from Urdu, and *ketchup* was borrowed from Chinese.

Words from African languages, too, made their way into English during the time that slavery was an institution in the United States. *Okra* (a vegetable) and *goober* (peanut) are examples.

The result of all of this absorption of new words is a very rich vocabulary that allows users of English to express subtlety of meaning and also formality and informality through their choice of words.

B Check the sentence in each pair that could belong in a summary of the passage.

1. ☐ English has borrowed many words from French and Latin, although these words are no longer considered foreign.

   ☐ The first two sentences in the first paragraph contain three words that were borrowed from French or Latin.

2. ☐ Food items have made their way into the English vocabulary – words such as *squash*, *tortilla*, *ketchup*, and *okra* were all borrowed from other languages.

   ☐ North American English has many words that were borrowed by early settlers from native populations and Spanish colonists.

C Now write a summary of the passage.

_____

_____

_____

_____

_____

_____

Lesson B   *Great communicators*

1

grammar

Choose the correct verb phrase to complete these sentences.

1. This candidate wants to be a legislator. He

   _____
   unsuccessfully to get elected five times. (has tried/
   has been tried)

2. He thinks that the government should let
   private businesses run the army. When he

   _____
   this position, half of the people started yelling.
   (explained/was explained)

3. When he said that the government

   _____
   the people more, the other half started shouting.
   (should tax/should be taxed)

4. If the sound system hadn't failed, his speech

   _____
   more successfully. (might have delivered/might have been delivered)

5. When that happened, all of the people _____ !
   (cheered/were cheered)

6. The audience _____ a chance to ask questions, but
   no one did. (offered/was offered)

7. Of course, most voters think that this candidate _____
   in the election – again! (will defeat/will be defeated)

2

grammar

Rewrite each sentence using the passive voice. Do not include the agent.

1. The company will offer me a high-paying job after I graduate.
   I will be offered a high-paying job after I graduate.

2. Many people have told me that I have good presentation skills.

   _____

3. Schools should teach foreign languages beginning in elementary school.

   _____

4. The language that people hear on the street these days is full of slang.

   _____

5. The linguist was carefully explaining the language theories to us.

   _____

6. My colleague reminded me to use eye contact during my speech.

   _____

7. The teacher would have given Brandon an A if he had worked harder on the final project.

   _____

Look at the pictures, and answer the questions using the passive form of the verbs given.

grammar

This isn't right. These directions are wrong.

This letter isn't clear, Jim. Please rewrite it.

1. Why is Penny lost?

   give <u>She was given the wrong</u>

   <u>directions.</u>

2. What is happening to Jim?

   tell _____

   _____

Where's the pizza? Is it all gone?

Don't forget to put on your jacket, Gregory.

3. Why was Lisa angry when she got home?

   eat _____

   _____

4. What has just happened to Gregory?

   remind _____

   _____

It's decided then. On Monday I'll ask if Jack wants the job.

5. What can Jack expect on Monday?

   offer _____

   _____

6. Why is Tetsuo frustrated?

   open _____

   _____

4

A Read this article. Find the underlined words that match these definitions.

1. express opinions in a strong, sure way _____*pontificate*_____
2. obstruction _____
3. the existing state of affairs _____
4. the highest level of things _____
5. value, worth _____

Dialects

Which of the following beliefs do you hold?
- There is a single standard variety of American English.
- Varieties of English that differ from the standard are considered substandard dialects.
- Official encouragement of more than one language is an **impediment** to national unity.

All of these beliefs about language are widely accepted, and they inform public discourse and public policy.

Nearly everyone has an opinion about language. "People would never **pontificate** about a physics issue," says Donna Christian, president of the Center for Applied Linguistics. "But they wouldn't hesitate to pontificate about language."

Examining what ordinary people believe to be true about language, a number of scholars say, allows us to identify some of the deeper impulses beneath the public battles: among them, fear of the unfamiliar, insistence on language "standards" as a way of preserving the social **status quo**, and the condemnation of "substandard" speech as a coded expression of prejudice against the speaker.

Judged on purely linguistic grounds, all languages and dialects have equal **merit**. All spring from the same human cognitive faculties; all have the same expressive potential and operate according to the same kinds of logical rule systems. Why, then, are some dialects considered substandard?

The answer is simple: judgments about relative worth are socially determined.

Many Americans believe there is a single standard dialect, but in reality, no one such creature exists. "If you said to anyone, 'Here's a room; put the hundred people in there you think speak the best English,' you'd get people that speak all different kinds of English," linguist Rosina Lippi-Green says.

But if we allow all these diverse Englishes into the **pantheon**, how can we keep out the ones that discomfort us, like African-American vernacular or working-class Brooklynese? That is where language myth comes in.

One function of myth, as Lippi-Green points out, is to provide a rationale for preserving the existing social order. The myths of standard and substandard English do just that, permitting those in power to label others inferior on the basis of their "broken" language.

B Read these statements. Are they supported by the information in the article? Check yes (**Y**) or no (**N**).

	Y	N
1. There is one standard variety of American English.	☐	☐
2. People often think that they are experts on language.	☐	☐
3. Some languages are inferior in terms of their expressiveness and logic.	☐	☐
4. Criticizing the kind of language that a person uses is sometimes a substitute for criticizing that person's social group.	☐	☐

Lesson A   Good science, bad science

1 vocabulary

Choose the correct word to complete these sentences.

1. The _____ of silicon as an electrical semitransistor led to the later development of microchips. (consequence/discovery/invention)

2. The _____ of the laser printer was possible only after several other technologies were in place. (discovery/invention/phenomenon)

3. Software producers have come to the _____ that many people work better with computers if the commands are visual and can be selected with a mouse. (conclusion/discovery/theory)

4. Employers have now taken notice of the _____ that constant use of computers can cause serious damage to employees' wrists. (phenomenon/law/invention)

5. One _____ of the computer age is that telecommuting is a viable option for many people. (consequence/phenomenon/theory)

6. In _____, the use of computers is supposed to reduce the amount of paper in people's lives. Some people now feel that this is incorrect. (conclusion/consequence/theory)

2 grammar

Check the sentences that use articles incorrectly, and then rewrite them.

1. ☑ For many people, using an abacus is an alternative to using calculator. *For many people, using an abacus is an alternative to using a calculator.*

2. ☐ Abacus is the earliest form of mechanical computing.

_____

3. ☐ The Chinese probably invented it more than five thousand years ago.

_____

4. ☐ It consists of wooden frame with wires that are strung together.

_____

5. ☐ On wires are beads, which represent units.

_____

6. ☐ Calculations are made by moving the beads up and down.

_____

7. ☐ Skilled operator can make calculations on it very quickly.

_____

8. ☐ It is still widely used in Asia and in the former Soviet Union.

_____

Complete these paragraphs with *a, an,* or *the.* Put an X where an article is not required.

grammar

_____The_____ digital camera is changing the way that people take _____ pictures. As with
  1   2
most new things, there are advantages and drawbacks to digital cameras.

Traditional cameras work by focusing _____ image onto light-sensitive film in the camera.
                                           3
To see the pictures, the photographer has to send _____ film to _____ company that
                                                        4   5
processes it. While this is _____ process that can take several days, _____ quality of the
                                6   7
pictures is reliable and usually very good.

Digital cameras use no film at all. Rather, they convert the light entering the camera into
_____ information such as that which can be read by _____ computer. In fact, if you
    8   9
have _____ computer, you can view your pictures on _____ screen. You can also send
         10   11
the pictures that you took to your friends over the Internet. Another advantage of _____
                                                                                        12
digital cameras is that you can see your work immediately. If you don't like _____ picture,
                                                                                  13
you can simply erase it by pressing _____ button.
                                         14
Some people think that _____ most serious problem with digital cameras is making
                            15
copies of the pictures. If you don't have _____ color printer, you are limited to sharing
                                               16
your pictures with others electronically. Also, unless the color printer is of very high quality,
_____ pictures won't look as good as if they were taken with _____ traditional camera.
    17   18

Write a sentence about each topic.

grammar

the most destructive weather phenomenon
the silliest invention I can think of
a medical cure I'd like to see discovered
a consequence of genetic engineering
the trendiest product on the market
the most interesting Web site
a principle I follow in my life

1. *I think the most destructive weather phenomenon is the tornado.* _____
2. _____
3. _____
4. _____
5. _____
6. _____
7. _____

writing

A Read these characteristics of traditional commerce and E-commerce (electronic commerce, or purchasing goods and services over the Internet). Then put them under the correct heading.

- Shopping takes place at home.
- You must carry cash or credit cards.
- Purchases will automatically be delivered.
- You can see the products in person.
- Shopping takes place in stores.
- You're able to hunt for bargains.
- You're able to do comparison shopping.
- There's a wide range of items to choose from.
- Your credit card number is always needed.
- You can often return items if you're unsatisfied.
- You see pictures and read about products.
- It's usual to carry your purchases home.

traditional commerce only

_____

_____

_____

_____

E-commerce only

_____

_____

_____

_____

_____

traditional commerce and E-commerce

_____

_____

_____

_____

_____

B What is your opinion of traditional commerce vs. E-commerce? Write a thesis statement expressing your opinion on the subject.

_____

_____

_____

_____

C Now write a comparison/contrast essay. Include your thesis statement in the introduction, two paragraphs describing the similarities and differences, and a conclusion restating your point of view.

Lesson B *Technology and you*

grammar

Read this paragraph and underline the verbs in the present perfect and present perfect continuous forms.

Scientists at Food Technologies, Inc., <u>have developed</u> a group of food plants that are resistant to insect damage and diseases. Although farmers have been planting these genetically engineered crops for years, it's not clear that consumers are ready to accept them. In some cities, shoppers have been gathering in the streets to protest genetically engineered food. Many of these people believe that the technology of genetic engineering needs to be carefully controlled, and a group of government officials has adopted this point of view. They have agreed that action needs to be taken and claim they will propose a new law soon. However, a spokeswoman for Food Technologies, Inc., has insisted that government involvement is unnecessary.

grammar

Complete each sentence with the present perfect or present perfect continuous form of each verb. Consider whether the action is completed or still going on.

1. The superintendent _____ my fire alarm. Now he's going to test it. (install)

2. Scientists from all over the world _____ to find a cure for cancer for many years. (try)

3. Ken _____ the lie detector test. He is no longer under any suspicion from the police. (pass)

4. Lucy _____ the VCR manual. She's now ready to set the timer. (study)

5. The clock on my microwave oven _____ on and off for days. (blink)

6. I _____ the research article. I can now discuss it with my classmates. (read)

7. Carol and I _____ since 10:00 for the telephone repairperson to come. We're willing to wait only one more hour. (wait)

grammar

Write a sentence stating either a positive or negative effect of each technology.

1. biotechnology _____

_____

2. animal cloning _____

_____

3. wireless communication _____

_____

4. satellite television _____

_____

Complete each sentence with the present perfect continuous form of the verb, if possible. If not, use the present perfect.

1. Many people _____*have had*_____ car accidents while using their cell phones. (have)

2. Professor Melon believes that he _____ a cure for baldness. (discover)

3. The salesman _____ on the front door for several minutes. (knock)

4. People _____ to develop alternative energy sources for some time. (try)

5. Televisions _____ smaller and smaller over the years. (become)

6. Scientists _____ for life in outer space for years. (search)

reading

A Read this article. Check the uses of soy products the article mentions.

☐ cosmetics ☐ food ☐ fuel ☐ ink ☐ lubricant ☐ medicine

The Soybean

Once a wild ground-crawling plant, today's soybean plant has been bred by Chinese farmers for more than three thousand years to grow upright. The typical plant now stands about three feet high and measures three feet wide.

For Asians who do not drink animal milk, the soybean quickly became indispensable. The beans were known as the "cow of China" because they were soaked in water to yield a white liquid now called soy milk. In 206 B.C., soybeans were first fermented to make *douchi*, the predecessor of soy sauce.

Around the seventh century, *miso* emerged in Japan, evolving in part from a soybean paste that Buddhist monks brought from China. Miso was made almost exclusively by monks, and remained a delicacy of the privileged upper classes until the tenth century.

The earliest references of Western visitors to China and Japan rarely mentioned the soybean.

Instead, travelers wrote of "gravy" (soy sauce), "great cakes like cheeses" (tofu), and "milk out of the kidney beans" (soy milk). Samuel Bowen, an American adventurer, is credited with having introduced the soybean to the United States in the mid-1700s. Over the next two hundred years, soy products went from relative obscurity to the basis of a burgeoning industry.

The oil embargoes and resulting shortages of the 1970s created a need for an alternative oil for making printers' inks. Today, nearly one third of American newspapers use soy-based inks. Researchers have also found applications for soybean oil as a clean-burning substitute for diesel fuel in city buses and as a machine lubricant.

In the 1990s, researchers began experimenting with genetically modified soybean plants. Some of the benefits of these "designer" plants are larger crop yields, higher-quality edible oil, greater protein content, and resistance to disease.

From its practical origins in ancient China, the soybean has journeyed far – a journey that may, in fact, have only just begun.

B How many of these statements are true? Check true (**T**) or false (**F**). Then rewrite the false statements to make them true.

	T	F
1. The soybean is a relatively new food crop.	☐	☐
2. Today's soy sauce has its origins in China.	☐	☐
3. Only monks enjoyed miso in Japan until the tenth century.	☐	☐
4. Soybeans are a major crop in the United States.	☐	☐
5. Most newspapers in the United States use soy-based ink.	☐	☐
6. The soybean is the focus of a great deal of technological experimentation and development.	☐	☐

Entrepreneurs

1

grammar

Read each sentence and then answer the questions.

1. If Janet hadn't lost her job at a bakery, she would never have considered starting her own business.

   Did Janet lose her job at the bakery? _____
   Did she consider starting her own business? _____

2. Had she known how difficult running a business would be, she probably wouldn't have started one.

   Did she know how difficult a business would be? _____
   Did she start a business? _____

3. Janet wouldn't have been able to spend a lot of time developing the business if she had had a large family.

   Was she able to spend a lot of time developing the business? _____
   Did she have a large family? _____

4. Janet's Cookies wouldn't have become the best-selling cookies in the city had she not worked so hard.

   Did Janet's Cookies become the best-selling cookies in the city? _____
   Did Janet work hard? _____

2

grammar

Complete these dialogs with the past perfect form of the verb, adding *not* when necessary.

1. A: Congratulations on your new business. I hear it's a great success.
   B: Thanks. If I _____*hadn't taken*_____ (take) this risk, I'm sure I would have been with my old job until retirement.

2. A: It's too bad Jerry didn't take your advice.
   B: I know. If he _____ (follow) my advice, he would have made a small fortune.

3. A: We missed you at this morning's meeting, Lynn.
   B: I'm sorry, but if I _____ (have) to meet with a new client, I would have been there.

4. A: Do you have any regrets about dropping out of medical school, Tom?
   B: Not really. If I _____ (stay) in, I wouldn't have been able to pay the tuition costs much longer anyway.

5. A: I hear you didn't have a lot of shoppers at your year-end sale.
   B: That's right. I'm certain more people would have come if I _____ (advertise) the sale on television.

6. A: I'm sorry to hear that your wife's flower shop has gone out of business.
   B: It's disappointing, but I think if she _____ (choose) a better location, she would have had more customers.

3

grammar

Write a sentence for each situation using a conditional clause (*Had . . . not . . .*).

1. *Had the woman not answered the ad, she* _____

2. _____

3. _____

4. _____

writing

A Read this business letter. There are three sentences that do not belong because they are too personal or irrelevant. Cross them out.

> 85 Sun Road
> Phoenix, AZ 85051
> September 13, 2000
>
> Ms. Deborah Moyers
> Quick Copy Center
> 4226 N. 22nd St.
> Phoenix, AZ 85016
>
> Dear Ms. Moyers:
>
> I am writing in response to the advertisement for a copy machine technician in last Sunday's Phoenix *Star*. I am very interested in the position and am enclosing my resume for your consideration. It is very kind of you to read this letter.
>
> I believe that I meet all of the qualifications that you specify. You have probably never had a candidate as qualified as I am! I have had five years of experience as a copy machine technician in a retail environment. I am trained in digital and color technology, and I have experience with all major brands of equipment.
>
> In addition to my technical skills, I enjoy training staff members and am very good with customers. None of my current customers wants me to leave.
>
> I would appreciate the opportunity to discuss this position with you in person. I look forward to hearing from you at your convenience.
>
> Sincerely,
>
> *James Ditzler*
> James Ditzler

B Imagine a job that you would be interested in applying for. Make notes on the following:

Why you want the position

_____

_____

_____

Your experience

_____

_____

_____

Why you should be considered

_____

_____

_____

C Use your notes to write a business letter applying for the job you are interested in.

Lesson B *The new worker*

grammar

Match these clauses to make conditional sentences.

1. As long as I had an opportunity to influence decisions, ____

2. On the condition my company paid for part of it, ____

3. Provided that the location was good, ____

4. Suppose your company offered you an early retirement package, ____

5. Unless you have a very good reason to change jobs, ____

a. I would consider opening my own restaurant.

b. I'd strongly recommend staying where you are.

c. do you think you would take it?

d. I would take a position at a smaller company.

e. I would go back to school in the evenings.

grammar

Respond to what the first speaker says in these conversations. Write sentences using the adverb clauses of condition provided.

1. A: If I were offered an interesting job that paid well, I would accept it right away.
   B: provided (that) *I would probably accept it, too, provided that the benefits were also good.*

   _____

2. A: If I had to commute to work on a daily basis, I would definitely do it. It can't be that much of an inconvenience.
   B: on the condition (that) _____

   _____

3. A: A lot of people think office jobs aren't interesting. I don't think that's true at all.
   B: as long as _____

   _____

4. A: Under no circumstances would I ever accept a demotion. No one should move down in a company.
   B: suppose (that) _____

   _____

5. A: If my boss said something in a meeting that I strongly disagreed with, I would definitely speak up.
   B: unless _____

   _____

6. A: I think that it's OK to lend a family member a large amount of money in order to start a business.
   B: provided (that) _____

   _____

3 grammar

Under what conditions would you do – or not do – these things? Write sentences using the expressions in the box.

> as long as
> on the condition (that)
> provided (that)
> unless

1. take a pay cut

   _____

2. work every weekend

   _____

3. be transferred to a different country

   _____

4. work two jobs at the same time

   _____

5. quit your job and go back to school

   _____

6. leave a good job to start your own business

   _____

4 vocabulary

Choose the quality that you consider to be the most important for each job. Then write a sentence explaining why.

1. doctor (conscientiousness/leadership/training)

   Training is the most important thing for doctors because people's lives are in their hands.

2. engineer (honesty/innovation/optimism)

   _____

3. politician (charisma/honesty/influence)

   _____

4. teacher (communication/self-control/training)

   _____

5. business executive (influence/initiative/leadership)

   _____

6. attorney (adaptability/conscientiousness/trustworthiness)

   _____

7. student (adaptability/initiative/self-control)

   _____

reading

A Read this article. Do you think all of these procedures are appropriate? Why or why not?

New Recruitment Procedures

Traditional recruiting procedures for attracting high-quality workers include background checks and face-to-face interviews. However, more and more employers are augmenting the usual screening methods with less conventional techniques. Although these procedures are used to weed out undesirable applicants, they also help to assess potential.

Reading minds and muscles

Although most tests assess behavioral patterns, others – such as biofeedback – are being used to assess the potential for injury on the job. Biofeedback, which assesses impulses from the brain to the muscles, can determine the validity of an injury and therefore the legitimacy of an insurance claim. The procedure also can detect vulnerabilities in people who are prone to injuries.

Handwriting analysis

Debbie Berk, president of Signature Dynamics, a handwriting analysis firm, says that 90% of her clients are managers seeking either to assess work potential or to analyze the behavior of current or potential employees. Although some people balk at using this method, it has been used to determine promotions or new hires at many companies. "I've had clients tell me they thought this was voodoo," Berk said. "But they have seen the validity in it and continue to use my services."

Watchdogs

Companies do not use these methods without oversight, however. The American Civil Liberties Union (ACLU) has a division that tracks both traditional and nontraditional screening procedures and files charges opposing those that appear to be discriminatory. Massachusetts, for example, now outlaws psychological testing in employee screening. The ACLU has argued that some tests contain questions irrelevant to job performance.

Insights

Many agree that one of the oldest recruitment methods – the interview – is still the best. The psychologist Vivian Lord has studied workplace behavior extensively. She notes that the best personality indicators are in the answers to an interviewer's questions. Consider the questions below and what the response (in parentheses) is meant to show.

▶ "Describe the best boss you ever had. Describe the worst boss you ever had." (Does the person claim "personality conflicts" to explain problems?)
▶ "Tell me about a failure in your life and why it occurred." (Does he or she take responsibility – or blame others?)
▶ "Describe a problem you had in which someone else's help was important to you." (Does he or she give the person credit or express appreciation?)

No one method works for every company. In order to recruit the best employees, a manager must choose screening procedures that reveal the behaviors most sought after – and most necessary to avoid – for his or her own department. The good news is, there are many to choose from.

B According to the information in the article, the following sentences are false. Rewrite them to make them true.

1. Biofeedback information is used to determine how intelligent job applicants are.

2. Handwriting analysis is widely accepted as a useful tool in assessing candidates.

3. The ACLU has rarely found unfairness in companies' recruitment practices.

4. The traditional interview is no longer considered to be a useful recruitment method.